P9-CQL-550

A to Z

BAR COOKIES

BAR COOKIES

by Marie Simmons

Photography by Susan Marie Anderson
Calligraphy by Richard High

CHAPTERS PUBLISHING LTD., SHELBURNE, VERMONT 05482

For Cassie and Evelyn,
Tiger and Zephyr

Thanks, to each of you, for keeping me company in the kitchen

Permissions

Date, Oatmeal & Walnut Bars, Carrot-Pecan Bars with Cream Cheese & Nutmeg Frosting, Figgy Bars, Peanut Butter-Chocolate Bars and Zebra Bars first appeared in slightly different form in the October 15, 1985 issue of *Woman's Day*. Reprinted by permission.

Copyright © 1994 by Marie Simmons
Photographs copyright © 1994 by Susan Marie Anderson
Calligraphy copyright © 1994 by Richard High

All rights reserved. No part of this book may be reproduced or transmitted in any form or by any electronic or mechanical means, including information storage and retrieval systems, without permission in writing from the Publisher, except for the inclusion of brief quotations in a review.

Published by
Chapters Publishing Ltd.
2031 Shelburne Road
Shelburne, Vermont 05482

Library of Congress Cataloging-in-Publication Data
Simmons, Marie.
A to Z bar cookies / by Marie Simmons; photography by Susan Marie Anderson; calligraphy by Richard High.
        p.   cm.
Includes index.
ISBN 1-881527-55-7: $12.95
1. Brownies (Cookery) I. Title.
TX772.S54 1994
641.8'653 — dc20   94-8086

Trade distribution by
Firefly Books Ltd.
250 Sparks Avenue
Willowdale, Ontario
Canada M2H 2S4

Printed and bound in China by
Toppan Printing

Designed by Susan McClellan

10 9 8 7 6 5 4 3 2

Acknowledgments

Although many colleagues and friends have been especially helpful
with this book, I am particularly grateful for the support and guidance of both
my editor, Rux Martin, and my agent, Judith Weber. I also wish to thank Gretchen
Semuskie for her thorough recipe testing and invaluable comments, Tamara Holt,
for being there whenever I have needed her, and Susan McClellan,
for designing such a charming book.

Introduction

NEARLY EVERY SATURDAY when I was a child, I would spend the afternoon helping my grandmother make cookies. Nana's kitchen was a warm and welcoming place. There were ruffled curtains on the windows, a rocking chair in the corner and a large, round table in the middle of the room, where we measured the flour and sugar, creamed the butter and rolled and cut out the cookie dough. While we worked side by side, we chatted about school and family, plotting and planning the days and weeks to come.

One of Nana's signature cookies—and my own very favorite—was a round cookie stuffed with dried fruits that looked like a miniature pie. Nana rolled out the cream-cheese dough, and it was my job to cut it into circles with a big biscuit cutter. The dough was rich and tender, and Nana carefully transferred half of the cut circles to the cookie sheets and topped each with a spoonful of the prune filling. Meanwhile, using a well-worn metal thimble dipped in flour, I cut smaller circles in the remaining rounds of dough. After Nana had set these in place over the filling, I would press the edges together with my fingertips. Our bake-a-thon of juggling cookie sheets and slipping cookies onto racks to cool lasted for hours. Finally, with all the cookies baked, we sipped weak tea with milk and munched on a fresh-from-the-oven chunky prune cookie, our reward for an afternoon well spent.

Now I have my own kitchen, but regrettably, no longer the time to spend whole afternoons baking. One day, nostalgic for the taste of Nana's cookies but pressed for time, I devised a streamlined version. Instead of rolling and cutting dozens of circles, I decided to roll out two squares of dough, spread one with the prune filling, top it with the second, bake it and cut it into bars. The resulting Cream-Cheese Pastry Bars with Prune Filling (page 34) were delicious, and although these bar cookies are a leap away from Nana's original, they are close in inspiration and can be made in less than an hour.

UNLIKE MOST BAKED GOODS, which require a strict formula in order to succeed, bar cookies lend themselves to countless improvisations. Before my kitchen becomes a frenzy of activity, my mind starts to brim with new ideas and tempting combinations. Will it be apples and pecans, cranberry and orange, coconut and lemon, or chocolate and espresso? Do I want the bars to be thick and gooey, or thin and crisp? Dense like fudge, crumbly like a cookie, or soft like a cake? Will I make one layer, two layers, or perhaps three? Should the bars be iced, or dusted with sugar? Do I want nuts sprinkled on the top? Almonds, macadamia nuts or pecans? Jam is a good idea. Maybe raspberry, strawberry or apricot? Should it go into the batter or be spread between two layers? Do I want the bars to be crunchy with oatmeal, or tender with cornstarch and confectioners' sugar? From Apricot & Toasted Almond Bars with Amaretto Glaze, Butterscotties and Cherry-Chocolate Truffle Bars, through Kahlúa Cheesecake Bars and Lemon Love Notes, to honey-flavored Yogi Bars and Zebras, striped with vanilla and chocolate, my imagination travels from A to Z.

Some of the bar cookies in this collection have been inspired by new ingredients that would have amazed Nana. While nibbling on some candied ginger one day, I imagined Ginger Shortbread, a thin, crisp, buttery bar with flecks of the ginger, an instant success. Tropical Rain Forest Crunch Bars imitate the flavors of a gourmet-store confection of cashews and brazil nuts that I adore. Other bars use familiar old ingredients that were staples in Nana's kitchen—pumpkin, jam and cream cheese—in new ways. Marmalade Brownies, Figgy Bars and Old-Fashioned Oatmeal & Raisin Bars reinvent traditional favorites. Island Gems, a scrumptious combination of caramelized sugar, cashews, macadamia nuts and coconut supported by a brown-sugar cookie base, were a lucky accident.

Because they are adaptable and virtually fail-proof, bar cookies are irresistible not only to the experienced and daring baker, but to the casual cook as well. I especially like their no-fuss, no-bother aspect. They are easier and neater than other cookies, which have to be rolled, molded or dropped from a spoon. To make them, you just mix the batter, spread it in a pan and pop it in the oven—no sticky fingers or blistering cookie sheets to contend with. Even the more complex layered bar cookies have an appealing simplicity.

But the most important feature of bar cookies is their versatility. They can be new and snappy, sophisticated and elegant, or as old-fashioned and familiar as your grand-mother's. And, of course, they are a joy to eat.

Baking Notes

1. For the recipes in this book, I use unsalted butter, large eggs and unbleached all-purpose flour.

2. Unless otherwise instructed, all ingredients normally stored in the refrigerator (eggs, butter, cream cheese, milk) should be used at room temperature. Remove them from the refrigerator about 30 minutes before using.

3. Butter should never be runny unless the recipe specifies it. Softened butter has been removed from the refrigerator about 30 minutes before using so that it is spreadable, as opposed to hard and cold.

4. Measure the flour by spooning it into metal or plastic dry measuring cups and leveling the top with a knife or spatula.

5. Usually, I measure the dry ingredients right into my sifter, which is set over a bowl or a piece of wax paper, and then sift all of the dry ingredients together to break up any bitter-tasting lumps of baking powder or baking soda. Wax paper makes a handy "funnel" for gradually adding the dry ingredients to the batter. If you do a lot of baking, fold up the wax paper and re-use it a couple of times.

6. Confectioners' sugar often gets lumpy in the package. I usually measure it (the way I measure flour) and then sift it before using.

7. Dark brown and light brown sugar can be used interchangeably and should always be packed when measured.

8. Traditionally, chocolate is melted in a double boiler over hot or barely simmering water. But as a shortcut, it can be melted carefully in a warm (never hot!) saucepan set over very, very low heat. To ensure even melting, chop the chocolate into small pieces and watch constantly until it begins to lose its shape. Chocolate scorches very quickly, so never take your

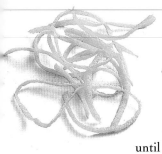

eyes off it while it is melting. Immediately remove the pan from the heat. Never allow the pan to get hot, only warm.

To melt chocolate in a microwave oven: Place in a small glass bowl and microwave on high for 1 to 2 minutes, stirring every 30 seconds, until the chocolate is smooth when stirred.

9. Semisweet and bittersweet chocolates are interchangeable in these recipes.

10. Always use glass or plastic calibrated measuring cups for liquids. Use standard measuring spoons. Remember that accuracy is always important in baking, so carefully level the surface with a knife or small spatula.

11. When cutting up dried fruits, lightly oil your knife, the blade of the food processor or scissors to prevent sticking and speed up the process.

12. When a recipe calls for orange or lemon zest, remember that the zest is the thin, fragrant, colorful portion of the rind only; it does not include the bitter white pith.

13. Most of the time, I brush the baking pan (bottom and sides) with a thin film of softened or melted butter. Another option is to use nonstick vegetable spray.

14. For even baking, position the rack in the center of the oven. If your oven bakes unevenly, turn the pan halfway through the baking time. I find that even if ovens are accurately calibrated, different ovens often give different results in varying amounts of time.

15. Bar cookies baked in a pan with a dull or dark surface will brown more quickly (and bake faster) than those baked in a pan with a shiny surface. Always check the bars 5 minutes before the recipe indicates they will be done to avoid overbaking, which will make the squares (especially those near the edges of the pan) dry.

16. Generally, bar cookies improve

with age. Many of these recipes actually taste better when they are a day old. They keep well at room temperature for about 5 days and freeze very well for a longer period of time. If any of these bar cookies are not good keepers, I say so in the introduction to the recipe.

Cutting the Bars

Be creative, if you wish, but after extensive experience, these are my favorite configurations:

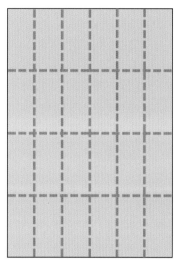

13-x-9-inch
PAN
24 BARS

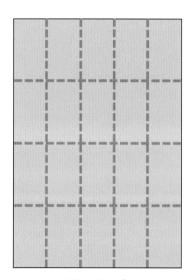

13-x-9-inch
PAN
20 BARS

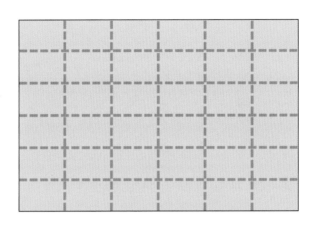

15-x-10-inch
PAN
36 BARS

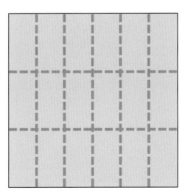

9-x-9-inch
PAN
18 BARS

Applesauce Bars

with Pecan Praline Topping

APPLESAUCE TENDS TO GIVE a "time-released" moistness to these bars, making them excellent keepers. In fact, the flavor and texture actually improve upon standing. Because I am partial to the crunchy sweetness of praline, I like to concoct brown sugar, butter and nut mixtures to sprinkle on top of my baked goods. You can easily substitute walnuts for the pecans in this recipe. Either works just fine.

Batter

¼ cup (½ stick) unsalted butter, softened

½ cup packed light brown sugar

1 large egg

1 teaspoon vanilla extract

1 cup chunky unsweetened applesauce

1½ cups unbleached all-purpose flour

1 teaspoon ground cinnamon

½ teaspoon baking powder

½ teaspoon baking soda

¼ teaspoon ground cloves

¼ teaspoon salt

1½ cups chopped, peeled, cored Golden Delicious apples

½ cup chopped pecans

Topping

⅔ cup packed light brown sugar

3 tablespoons unsalted butter, softened

1 tablespoon unbleached all-purpose flour

1 cup chopped pecans

1. Preheat the oven to 350 degrees F. Lightly butter a 13-x-9-inch baking pan.

2. **To make the Batter:** In a large bowl, beat together the butter and brown sugar with an electric mixer until light and fluffy. Add the egg and vanilla; beat until blended. Stir in the applesauce just until blended. (The mixture will look curdled.)

3. Sift together the flour, cinnamon, baking powder, baking soda, cloves and salt. Stir the dry ingredients into the butter mixture just until blended. Fold in the apples and the pecans. Spread the batter in the prepared pan.

4. **To make the Topping:** In a bowl, combine the brown sugar, butter and flour and blend with a fork; stir in the pecans until blended. Crumble the mixture evenly over the top of the batter.

5. Bake on the center rack for 30 to 35 minutes, or until the edges begin to pull away from the sides of the pan. Cool on a wire rack before cutting into bars.

MAKES 24 BARS

Apricot &
Toasted Almond Bars
with Amaretto Glaze

T HESE MULTILAYERED BARS are sophisticated: The cooked dried apricot filling is flavored with Amaretto liqueur and spread over a delicate cookie crust. Make them a day ahead and let them mellow, covered, for a day before cutting and serving.

Filling

1   **6-ounce package (1 cup) dried apricots**
1   **cup water**
¼   **cup Amaretto liqueur**
1   **drop almond extract**
1   **cup whole natural (unblanched) almonds**

Crust

2¼   **cups unbleached all-purpose flour**
¼   **cup packed light brown sugar**
    Pinch of salt
¾   **cup (1½ sticks) cold unsalted butter, cut into small pieces**
2   **large egg yolks**
1   **teaspoon vanilla extract**
½   **teaspoon almond extract**

Glaze

¾   **cup confectioners' sugar**
3   **tablespoons Amaretto liqueur**

1. **To make the Filling:** Combine the apricots and water in a medium saucepan. Heat to simmering over low heat; cover and cook until tender and most of the liquid is absorbed, about 15 minutes. Remove from the heat; set aside to cool, uncovered. Gradually stir in the

Amaretto until blended; add the almond extract. Set the filling aside.

2. Preheat the oven to 350 degrees F. Spread the almonds in a shallow pan and bake until golden, about 8 minutes. Set the nuts aside to cool; leave the oven on. Finely grind half of the toasted almonds in a food processor; set them aside for the crust. Coarsely chop the remaining toasted almonds; set them aside for the topping.

3. Lightly butter the bottom and sides of a 13-x-9-inch baking pan.

4. **To make the Crust:** In the bowl of a food processor, combine the finely ground almonds, flour, brown sugar and salt. With the motor running, add the butter, a few pieces at a time, through the feed tube until the mixture is crumbly. Stir together the egg yolks, vanilla and almond extract in a small bowl; with the motor running, add the egg mixture and process for a few seconds, or until the mixture begins to form a ball.

5. Measure out 2½ cups of the crust mixture and press it into the prepared pan; reserve the remaining crust mixture. Bake until golden, for 10 to 15 minutes. Remove from the oven and cool slightly.

6. Spread the apricot filling in a thin, even layer over the crust. Add the reserved chopped almonds to the remaining crust mixture. Squeeze the mixture in your hands to make clumps and sprinkle them over the filling, pressing down lightly with your fingertips. Bake for 25 minutes, or until the bars are lightly browned. Glaze the bars while still warm.

7. **To make the Glaze:** Sift the confectioners' sugar into a small bowl; add the Amaretto; stir until smooth. Drizzle over the warm bar cookies. Cool thoroughly before cutting into bars.

MAKES 24 BARS

Blueberry & Lemon Crumb Bars

I LIKE TO MAKE these bars in midsummer when the blueberry crop is at its peak, but frozen berries may be used; the bars will be a little more moist. As these bars bake, the butter crust, sugared blueberries and brown-sugar crumb topping melt together. The result is a just-sweet-enough fruit bar that is perfect with a tall glass of lemonade or iced tea.

Crust

1½ cups unbleached all-purpose flour
2 tablespoons sugar
2 teaspoons grated lemon zest
¼ teaspoon salt
½ cup (1 stick) cold unsalted butter, cut into ¼-inch pieces
1 large egg yolk
1 teaspoon vanilla extract
1 tablespoon cold water (optional)

Filling

½ cup sugar
2 tablespoons unbleached all-purpose flour
¼ teaspoon freshly grated nutmeg
2 cups blueberries, rinsed and picked over

Topping

5 tablespoons unsalted butter, softened
½ cup packed light brown sugar
¾ cup unbleached all-purpose flour
Confectioners' sugar

1. Preheat the oven to 400 degrees F. Lightly butter a 13-x-9-inch baking pan.

2. **To make the Crust:** Combine the flour, sugar, lemon zest and salt in the bowl of a food processor. With the motor running, add the butter, a few pieces at a time. In a small cup, stir together the egg yolk and vanilla. With the motor running, gradually add the yolk mixture through the feed tube; process until the mixture pulls together. If the mixture seems dry, add the cold water. Turn the dough out (it will be crumbly) into the prepared pan; with floured fingertips, carefully press the dough into an even layer over the bottom of the pan.

3. **To make the Filling:** In a large bowl, stir together the sugar, flour and nutmeg until blended. Add the blueberries; stir to coat. Spread the blueberry-and-sugar mixture into an even layer over the crust.

4. **To make the Topping:** Work the butter and sugar together with a wooden spoon until blended. Using a fork, gradu-

ally add the flour, stirring until the mixture resembles coarse crumbs. Sprinkle the mixture evenly over the blueberries.

5. Bake for 15 minutes. Reduce the oven temperature to 350 degrees, and bake for 25 to 30 minutes longer, or until the edges and topping are browned and the blueberries are cooked. Cool on a wire rack before cutting into bars. Sprinkle with confectioners' sugar before serving.

MAKES 24 BARS

Bourbon & Maple Bars

CRAZY FOR MAPLE SYRUP? Then you will love these bars, which are slightly chewy, with a hit of bourbon. They keep well—that is, if you hide them away somewhere. Make sure to use pure maple syrup, not maple-flavored pancake syrup variety.

Batter

2 cups unbleached all-purpose flour

1 teaspoon baking powder

1 cup (2 sticks) unsalted butter, softened

1 cup packed light brown sugar

2 large eggs

1 teaspoon vanilla extract

1 cup maple syrup

2 tablespoons bourbon

1 cup chopped pecans or walnuts

Glaze

1 cup confectioners' sugar

2 tablespoons maple syrup

2 tablespoons bourbon

1. Preheat the oven to 350 degrees F. Lightly butter a 13-x-9-inch baking pan.

2. **To make the Batter:** Sift together the flour and baking powder; set aside. In a large bowl, cream the butter and brown sugar with an electric mixer until light. Gradually beat in the eggs and vanilla until blended. Combine the maple syrup and bourbon; add in a slow, steady stream, beating gently until blended.

3. Stir in the flour mixture until blended. Add the pecans or walnuts; stir to blend.

4. Spread the batter in the prepared pan. Bake for 35 minutes, or until the edges begin to pull away from the sides of the pan. Cool on a wire rack, and glaze the bars while still warm.

5. **To make the Glaze:** Sift the confectioners' sugar into a small bowl. In a separate bowl, stir together the maple syrup and bourbon. Add the liquids to the confectioners' sugar, stirring until smooth. Drizzle the glaze over the warm bar cookies, spreading it into a thin, even layer. Cool thoroughly before cutting into bars.

MAKES 24 BARS

Butterscotties

T HESE ARE MOIST, chewy and decadent—very similar to the classic blondie, or butter-scotch "brownie" that is made with butterscotch chips and not a trace of chocolate. If you miss the chocolate, add it by simply sprinkling a layer of chocolate chips over the batter before the bars are baked. The chips will sink into the surface of the bars as they bake.

2¼	cups unbleached all-purpose flour	2	large eggs
1	teaspoon baking powder	2	teaspoons vanilla extract
½	teaspoon salt	1½	cups coarsely chopped walnuts
1	cup (2 sticks) unsalted butter, softened	½	cup butterscotch chips
1¾	cups packed light brown sugar	½	cup semisweet chocolate chips (optional)

1. Preheat the oven to 350 degrees F. Lightly butter a 13-x-9-inch baking pan.

2. Sift together the flour, baking powder and salt; set aside. In a large bowl, cream the butter and brown sugar with an electric mixer until light. Beat in the eggs, one at a time, beating well after each addition. Add the vanilla. Stir in the sifted dry ingredients, the walnuts and butterscotch chips until blended.

3. Spread in the prepared pan. Sprinkle the top with the chocolate chips, if using. Bake for 30 to 35 minutes, or until the edges begin to brown and pull away from the sides of the pan. Cool on a wire rack before cutting into bars.

MAKES 24 BARS

Carrot-Pecan Bars
with Cream Cheese & Nutmeg Frosting

I CREATED THIS RECIPE from my favorite carrot cake. It took a couple of experiments before the transformation from cake to bars was complete, but it was certainly worth the effort. Flecked with pieces of carrot and laced with lots of spice, the bars have a texture that is nicely balanced between a cake and a chewy cookie. Use freshly grated nutmeg, if at all possible, in the frosting.

Batter

1 cup unbleached all-purpose flour
½ cup whole-wheat flour
1 teaspoon ground cinnamon
½ teaspoon baking powder
½ teaspoon freshly grated nutmeg
½ teaspoon salt
½ cup finely chopped pecans
¾ cup vegetable oil
1 cup packed light brown sugar
2 large eggs
1 teaspoon vanilla extract
2 cups carrots, cut into ½-inch pieces

Frosting

2 3-ounce packages cream cheese, softened
1 cup confectioners' sugar, sifted
1 tablespoon fresh lemon juice
½ teaspoon freshly grated nutmeg
½ teaspoon vanilla extract

2 tablespoons finely chopped pecans

1. Preheat the oven to 350 degrees F. Lightly butter a 13-x-9-inch baking pan.

2. **To make the Batter:** Combine the flours, cinnamon, baking powder, nutmeg and salt in a large bowl; add the pecans; stir to blend.

3. Place the oil, brown sugar, eggs and vanilla in the bowl of a food processor. Process until blended. With the motor running, gradually add the carrots through the feed tube; process until the carrots are finely chopped. Pour the carrot mixture over the dry ingredients; stir until well blended.

4. Spread the batter in the prepared pan. Bake for 35 minutes, or until the edges pull away from the sides of the pan. Cool on a wire rack.

5. **To make the Frosting:** Beat the cream cheese and confectioners' sugar until smooth. Add the lemon juice, nutmeg and vanilla.

6. Spread the frosting over the cooled bars. Sprinkle with the finely chopped pecans. Let stand for about 1 hour before cutting into bars.

MAKES 24 BARS

Cherry-Chocolate Truffle Bars

T HESE BARS ARE WET and chewy, more candy than cookie. Dried cherries are addictive little gems, and when you look at the price, you really may consider them jewels. But they are lovely when eaten with chocolate and worth every cent.
Tip: To chop dried cherries (or any dried fruit for that matter), brush the blade of the food processor lightly with oil to discourage sticking. Dried tart red cherries are available by mail-order from American Spoon Foods, P.O. Box 566, Petoskey, Michigan 49770; (800) 222-5886.

¾ cup hazelnuts (filberts)
4 large eggs
2 cups packed light brown sugar
2 teaspoons vanilla extract
¾ cup (1½ sticks) cold unsalted butter, cut into pieces
4 1-ounce squares unsweetened chocolate

1 cup unbleached all-purpose flour
½ teaspoon salt
¾ cup chopped dried tart red cherries
¾ cup semisweet chocolate chips

1. Preheat the oven to 350 degrees F. Place the hazelnuts in a baking pan and bake until the skins are split and the nuts are golden, 10 to 15 minutes. Transfer to a large dish towel; leave the oven on. Rub the nuts vigorously to remove the loosened skins. Separate the nuts from the skins and coarsely chop; set aside.

2. Lightly butter a 13-x-9-inch baking pan.

3. In a large bowl, combine the eggs and brown sugar. Beat with an electric mixer for 10 minutes, or until the mixture is light and fluffy. Meanwhile, melt the butter and the chocolate in a small saucepan over low

31

heat, stirring frequently. (Or place them in a heatproof bowl and microwave on high, stirring every 30 seconds, until melted, about 2 minutes.) Cool slightly.

4. Slowly beat the chocolate mixture into the egg mixture; add the flour and salt; stir until blended. Stir in the hazelnuts and the dried cherries.

5. Spread the batter in the prepared pan. Sprinkle the chocolate chips evenly over the surface. Bake for 30 to 35 minutes, or until the edges begin to pull away from the sides of the pan. Cool on a wire rack before cutting into bars.

MAKES 24 BARS

Chocolate-Frosted Chocolate Espresso Bars

T HESE EXCEPTIONALLY easy-to-make cookies are dedicated to my husband, John, because he requested an espresso bar. Sip a cup of fresh-brewed espresso while nibbling on this deep chocolate, chocolate-frosted, espresso-laced cookie.

Batter
½ cup unbleached all-purpose flour

⅓ cup imported or European-style unsweetened cocoa powder

2 tablespoons plus 2 teaspoons powdered instant espresso coffee

¼ teaspoon baking powder

¼ teaspoon salt

½ cup (1 stick) unsalted butter, cut into ½-inch pieces

1 cup packed light brown sugar

1 teaspoon vanilla extract

2 large eggs

¾ cup chopped pecans or walnuts

Frosting

¼ cup (½ stick) unsalted butter

¾ cup semisweet chocolate chips

⅓ cup milk

½ teaspoon vanilla extract

½ cup confectioners' sugar, sifted

1. Preheat the oven to 350 degrees F. Lightly butter a 13-x-9-inch baking pan.

2. **To make the Batter:** Sift together the flour, cocoa powder, espresso powder, baking powder and salt; set aside.

3. In a medium saucepan, heat the butter over low heat until melted. Remove from the heat. With a wooden spoon, stir in the brown sugar and vanilla until blended. Add the eggs, one at a time, beating well with the wooden spoon after each addition.

4. Gradually stir in the sifted dry ingredients until blended. Stir in the nuts.

5. Spread the batter evenly in the prepared baking pan. Bake for 20 to 25 minutes, or until the edges begin to pull away from the sides of the pan. Do not overbake. Cool on a wire rack.

6. **To make the Frosting:** Melt the butter and chocolate chips in a small saucepan over very low heat; remove from the heat. (Or place in a heatproof bowl and microwave on high, stirring every 30 seconds, until melted, about 2 minutes.) Stir in the milk, vanilla and confectioners' sugar until smooth. Refrigerate until cold, about 45 minutes. Beat with a wooden spoon until light and stiff enough to spread.

7. Spread the icing on the cooled bars. Let stand until the icing sets, about 1 hour. Cut into bars.

MAKES 24 BARS

Cream-Cheese Pastry Bars
with Prune Filling

THESE WERE INSPIRED by two favorite cookies: one, the classic Jewish sweet, Haman-taschen, a cream-cheese pastry filled with dried fruit, honey and poppy seeds; and the other, a chunky prune-filled cookie that my grandmother used to make. These bars turned out to be dainty and delicate, quite different from their inspirations. For the filling, I use a mixture of cooked prunes, walnuts and orange zest. The pastry, light with butter and cream cheese, is easily made in a food processor.

Pastry

4 ounces (half of an 8-ounce package) cream cheese, cut into small pieces and softened

½ cup (1 stick) unsalted butter, cut into small pieces and softened

1 cup unbleached all-purpose flour

2 tablespoons sugar
   Pinch of salt

Filling

1 cup pitted prunes, snipped with scissors

½ cup fresh orange juice or water

1 teaspoon grated orange zest

¼ cup finely chopped walnuts

1 large egg, beaten
   Confectioners' sugar

1. **To make the Pastry:** Place the cream cheese, butter, flour, sugar and salt in the bowl of a food processor. Process just until a dough begins to form. Turn out onto a floured surface and gather into a ball. Place on a piece of plastic wrap, flatten slightly, wrap and refrigerate for at least 2 hours, or until chilled.

2. Meanwhile, **make the Filling:** Combine the prunes and orange juice or water in a small nonaluminum saucepan. Cover and cook over low heat until the prunes absorb all of the moisture, about 15 minutes. Cool slightly. Place in a food processor and process until the consistency is fairly smooth. Transfer to a bowl and stir in the orange zest and walnuts. Set aside until ready to use.

3. Preheat the oven to 400 degrees F. Cut a piece of foil to fit the bottom of a 9-inch square pan. Place the foil on a work surface. Lightly butter the pan.

4. Remove the chilled pastry from the refrigerator and divide in half. Place one half in the center of the foil and, using a lightly floured rolling pin, roll out the dough to fit the foil. Trim the edges flush with the foil, as needed, and use the trimmings to patch the rounded corners and make them square, trimming with a small knife, as needed. Invert the foil into the prepared pan; carefully peel off the foil. Reserve the foil for the remaining pastry.

5. Spread the pastry-lined pan with a thin, even layer of the prune filling. Roll out the remaining half of the pastry as described in Step 4 above. Invert the pastry over the filling; peel off the foil. Lightly brush the top of the pastry with the beaten egg.

6. Bake for 5 minutes. Reduce the heat to 350 degrees and bake for 25 minutes, or until the top is golden and the edges have pulled away from the sides of the pan. Cool on a wire rack. Dust the top with confectioners' sugar sifted through a small strainer. Cut into bars.

MAKES 18 BARS

Date, Oatmeal & Walnut Bars

T HE CONTRAST of the soft date and orange filling, the crunchy cookie crust and the crumb topping strikes just the right balance in these bars. Because the crust and topping are the same mixture, these bar cookies are especially easy to whip together and get into the oven. The date filling can be made ahead and kept on hand in the refrigerator. It keeps for at least one week or more.

Filling

1	**8-ounce package dates, chopped or diced (about 2 cups)**
½	**cup dark raisins**
1	**cup water**
1	**teaspoon grated orange zest**
1	**teaspoon vanilla extract**

Crust & Topping

2	**cups unbleached all-purpose flour**
1	**cup old-fashioned oatmeal**

½	**cup packed light brown sugar**
½	**cup finely chopped walnuts**
1	**teaspoon ground cinnamon**
½	**teaspoon salt**
1	**cup (2 sticks) cold unsalted butter, cut into pieces**
1	**large egg yolk**
1	**teaspoon vanilla extract**

Confectioners' sugar

1. **To make the Filling:** Combine the dates, raisins, water and orange zest in a medium saucepan. Heat to boiling; cook over low heat, uncovered, until the dates are tender and the water is absorbed, about 15 minutes. Cool. Stir in the vanilla extract. Set the filling aside.

2. Preheat the oven to 350 degrees F. Lightly butter a 13-x-9-inch baking pan.

3. **To make the Crust and Topping:** In a large bowl, combine the flour, oatmeal, brown sugar, walnuts, cinnamon and salt. Add the butter and cut in with a pastry blender or 2 knives until the mixture is crumbly. In a small bowl, stir together the egg yolk and vanilla. Add to the flour mixture and toss with a fork to blend. Rub the mixture with your fingertips to distribute the ingredients evenly.

4. Measure out 2½ cups of the crust mixture and press it into the prepared pan in a thin, even layer. Drop spoonfuls of the filling evenly over the crust. Gently spread in a thin layer with a small flexible spatula. Sprinkle the remaining crust mixture evenly over the top; press down lightly with your fingertips.

5. Bake for 35 minutes, or until the edges begin to brown. Cool on a wire rack before cutting into bars. Sprinkle with confectioners' sugar.

MAKES 24 BARS

Dark Ginger Bars
with Dark Chocolate Frosting

MOIST, DARK AND RICH with flavor, these bars are cakelike and dark brown like an intense gingerbread. The ginger is added in three forms: dried, freshly grated, and pureed and preserved in sugar syrup (see Sources on the facing page). Inspired by a ginger cake in *The Birthday Cake Book*, by Sylvia Thompson, I have added a chocolate frosting. But these are great plain or frosted.

Batter

2¼	cups unbleached all-purpose flour
2	teaspoons ground ginger
2	teaspoons baking soda
½	teaspoon salt
¾	cup (1½ sticks) unsalted butter, softened
1	cup packed dark brown sugar
½	cup unsulphured dark molasses

1	large egg
½	cup grated fresh ginger
2	tablespoons pureed ginger in syrup

Frosting

½	cup heavy cream
6	1-ounce squares semisweet or bittersweet chocolate, coarsely chopped

1. Preheat the oven to 350 degrees F. Lightly butter a 13-x-9-inch baking pan.

2. **To make the Batter:** Sift the flour, ground ginger, baking soda and salt together; set aside. In a large bowl, cream together the butter and brown sugar with an electric mixer until light and fluffy; add the molasses and egg; beat until blended.

3. Add the sifted dry ingredients to the creamed mixture. Stir with a wooden spoon until blended. Add the grated fresh ginger and the ginger puree in syrup and stir to blend.

4. Spoon the batter into the prepared baking pan and spread into an even layer. Bake for about 25 minutes, or until the edges begin to pull away from the sides of the pan. (The surface will be uneven but should level as the bars cool.) Cool in the pan.

5. **To make the Frosting:** Heat the heavy cream in a small, heavy saucepan until boiling; remove from the heat. Stir in the chocolate until melted and smooth. Cool, stirring occasionally, until thick enough to spread, about 1 hour. Spread the bars with the chocolate frosting, and let set for at least 4 hours before cutting into bars.

MAKES 24 BARS

Ginger Sources: Peel the fresh ginger and grate it by hand or pulverize it in a food processor or chopper. Freshly grated ginger and pureed ginger in syrup are available in vacuum-sealed packages in some supermarkets. To make pureed ginger in syrup, purchase stem ginger in syrup, chop into small pieces and puree in a food processor.

Dried Fruit & Molasses Bars

THESE BARS HAVE a deep, dark molasses flavor; the pieces of dried apricots, prunes and raisins add a pleasant chewiness. Wrapped individually in plastic wrap, these bars age especially well.

1½ cups unbleached all-purpose flour
½ teaspoon baking soda
  Pinch of salt
1 cup chopped walnuts
1 cup snipped (½-inch pieces) pitted prunes

½ cup snipped (½-inch pieces) dried apricots
½ cup dark raisins
½ cup (1 stick) unsalted butter, softened
1 cup packed dark brown sugar
1 large egg
½ cup unsulphured molasses

1. Preheat the oven to 350 degrees F. Lightly butter a 13-x-9-inch baking pan.
2. Sift together the flour, baking soda and salt. Combine the walnuts, prunes, apricots and raisins in a large bowl; add 2 tablespoons of the dry ingredients; stir to coat the dried fruits and nuts. Set aside.
3. Cream the butter and brown sugar with an electric mixer until light. Beat in the egg until blended. Gradually beat in the molasses on low speed, just until blended. Gradually beat in the dry ingredients until blended. Using a spatula, fold in the floured dried fruits and nuts until blended.
4. Spread the batter in the prepared pan. Bake for 30 minutes, or until the edges begin to pull away from the sides of the pan. Cool on a wire rack before cutting into bars.

MAKES 24 BARS

Energy Bars

G UARANTEED TO GIVE YOU an energy surge when you most need it, these mighty
morsels pack four grains: barley, oats, rye and wheat, plus dried fruits, nuts and seeds.

2 cups uncooked Quaker Multi-Grain cereal

½ cup dark raisins

½ cup snipped (½-inch pieces) pitted prunes

½ cup coarsely chopped whole natural (unblanched) almonds

½ cup unsalted sunflower seeds

1¼ cups unbleached all-purpose flour

2 teaspoons ground cinnamon

1 teaspoon baking soda

½ teaspoon salt

½ cup vegetable oil

⅔ cup packed light brown sugar

1 large egg

1 cup unsweetened applesauce

2 teaspoons vanilla extract

1. Preheat the oven to 350 degrees F. Lightly butter a 13-x-9-inch baking pan.

2. Combine the cereal, raisins, prunes, almonds, sunflower seeds, flour, cinnamon, baking soda and salt in a large bowl.

3. In a separate bowl, whisk the vegetable oil, brown sugar and egg until blended. Add the applesauce and vanilla; stir to blend. Add the dry ingredients and stir just until blended.

4. Spread the batter in the prepared pan. Bake for 35 to 40 minutes, or until golden brown. Cool until lukewarm on a wire rack before cutting into bars. These are good served warm from the oven.

MAKES 24 BARS

Figgy Bars

SUPERMARKET-VARIETY Fig Newtons were a childhood staple. These are the ultimate adult fig bar: a tender, buttery crust with a thick, moist fig filling flavored with vanilla extract. They keep well, so although this is a fairly big batch, wrap each individual bar in plastic wrap and keep on hand for lunch bags, tote bags and flight bags. They make a great quick hit when you need nutrient-dense energy. Calimyrna figs come from California and are found in the dried-fruit section of supermarkets.

Filling

2   8-ounce packages dried Calimyrna figs
2   cups water
2   teaspoons vanilla extract

Crust

2½   cups unbleached all-purpose flour
1½   teaspoons baking powder
1   teaspoon ground cinnamon
½   teaspoon salt
½   cup (1 stick) unsalted butter, softened
1   cup sugar
2   large eggs

1. **To make the Filling:** Using kitchen scissors, snip the stems off the figs; discard. Cut the figs in half. Combine the figs and water in a medium saucepan; heat to boiling. Lower the heat and simmer the figs, uncovered, for 25 minutes, or until the water is absorbed and the figs are tender. Cool slightly. Puree the figs in a food processor; add the vanilla extract. Set aside.

2. Preheat the oven to 350 degrees F. Lightly butter a 13-x-9-inch baking pan.

3. **To make the Crust:** Sift together the flour, baking powder, cinnamon and salt. Cream the butter and sugar together with an electric mixer until light and fluffy. Add the eggs, one at a time, beating well after each addition. Gently beat in the dry ingredients. With floured hands, gather the dough into a ball. Place on a sheet of wax paper and flatten into a disc. Wrap and refrigerate for at least 1 hour, or until chilled enough to roll.

4. Divide the dough in half. On a lightly floured surface, roll out half of the dough into a 13-x-9-inch rectangle. Trim the edges exactly with a sharp knife. Drape the dough over the rolling pin and transfer to the prepared pan. Patch any tears by pressing the dough together with floured fingertips.

5. Spoon the cooled fig mixture over the dough and spread out into a thin, even layer with a small flexible spatula. Roll out the remaining dough on a piece of wax paper to a 13-x-9-inch rectangle. Trim the edges exactly with a sharp knife. Lifting the dough on the wax paper, place it, paper side up, on top of the fig filling. Carefully peel off the paper. Don't worry if the dough tears. Patch any tears by pressing the dough together with your fingertips.

6. Bake for 30 minutes, or until the edges are golden. Cool on a wire rack before cutting into bars.

MAKES 24 BARS

Ginger Shortbread

F ILLED WITH BITS of sweet-hot crystallized ginger, these buttery cookie bars are a must for ginger fans — great with a cup of tea.

2¼ cups unbleached all-purpose flour

½ cup packed light brown sugar

1 tablespoon ground ginger

½ teaspoon baking powder

½ teaspoon salt

1 cup (2 sticks) unsalted butter, cut into ½-inch pieces and slightly softened

½ cup finely chopped crystallized ginger

1. Preheat the oven to 350 degrees F. Lightly butter a 13-x-9-inch baking pan.

2. Combine the flour, brown sugar, ginger, baking powder and salt in a mixing bowl. Add the butter and cut in with a pastry blender or 2 knives until the mixture makes fine crumbs. Add the crystallized ginger and stir with a fork to blend evenly.

3. With lightly floured fingertips, press the mixture into the prepared baking pan in an even layer over the bottom. Bake on the center rack for about 20 minutes, or until the edges are lightly browned. Cool in the pan on a wire rack before cutting into bars.

MAKES 24 BARS

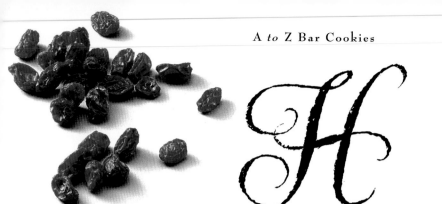

Hermits

I've SEEN DOZENS of recipes for hermits, no two exactly alike. The following one, full of the requisite nuts, raisins and cinnamon and sweetened with maple, is mine. The icing is optional, but it helps to keep the bars moist.

Batter

3	cups unbleached all-purpose flour
2	teaspoons ground cinnamon
1	teaspoon baking powder
½	teaspoon salt
1	cup coarsely chopped walnuts
1	cup dark raisins
½	cup golden raisins
1	cup (2 sticks) unsalted butter, softened
2	cups packed light brown sugar

3	large eggs
½	cup maple syrup
2	teaspoons vanilla extract

Icing

2½	cups confectioners' sugar
6-8	tablespoons half-and-half or heavy cream
1	teaspoon vanilla extract or ½ teaspoon maple flavoring

1. Preheat the oven to 350 degrees F. Lightly butter a 15-x-10-x-1-inch baking pan.

2. **To make the Batter:** Sift together the flour, cinnamon, baking powder and salt; set

aside. Combine the walnuts and the dark and golden raisins in a bowl. Add about 1 tablespoon of the flour mixture; toss to coat. Set aside.

3. In a large bowl, beat the butter and brown sugar with an electric beater until light and fluffy. Add the eggs, one at a time, beating well after each addition. Gradually beat in the maple syrup; add the vanilla.

4. Gradually stir in the flour mixture until blended. Fold in the dried fruits and nuts.

5. Spread the batter in the prepared pan. Bake for 25 to 30 minutes, or until the edges turn golden and begin to pull away from the sides of the pan. Cool on a wire rack.

6. **To make the Icing:** Sift the confectioners' sugar into a bowl. Gradually stir in 6 tablespoons of the half-and-half or cream until the mixture is thick and smooth. Add the vanilla or maple flavoring. Add more cream, if needed, to make a smooth, spreadable consistency. Spread the cooled bars with the icing and let set for about 1 to 2 hours before cutting into bars.

MAKES
36
BARS

Honey Granola Bars

RATHER THAN USING a prepackaged granola mixture for these bars, I put together my own formula of toasted oatmeal, wheat germ, nuts, seeds, dried fruits and coconut. The bars are crunchy and chewy at the same time and improve with age. Make them a day or two ahead; wrap tightly and dole them out a few at a time.

1½ cups old-fashioned oatmeal
1½ cups unbleached all-purpose flour
¼ cup toasted wheat germ
1 teaspoon baking powder
1 teaspoon ground cinnamon
½ teaspoon salt
½ cup snipped (½-inch pieces) dried apple slices
½ cup dark raisins
½ cup chopped natural (unblanched) almonds
½ cup flaked sweetened coconut
¼ cup toasted sunflower seeds
2 tablespoons sesame seeds

1 cup (2 sticks) unsalted butter, softened
½ cup packed dark brown sugar
2 large eggs
½ cup honey
2 teaspoons vanilla extract

1. Preheat the oven to 350 degrees F. Lightly butter a 13-x-9-inch baking pan.

2. Place the oatmeal in a dry skillet set over medium heat, and lightly toast, stirring constantly, about 4 minutes. Cool.

3. In a large bowl, combine the toasted oatmeal, flour, wheat germ, baking powder, cinna-

mon and salt. Add the snipped apple slices, raisins, almonds, coconut, sunflower seeds and sesame seeds; stir to blend.

4. In a separate large bowl, cream together the butter and brown sugar with an electric mixer until light and fluffy. Add the eggs, one at a time, beating well after each addition. Beat in the honey and vanilla until blended. Gradually add the dry ingredients to the batter, stirring until thoroughly blended.

5. Spread the mixture in the prepared pan. Bake for 35 minutes, or until the edges just begin to pull away from the sides of the pan. Cool on a wire rack before cutting into bars.

MAKES 24 BARS

Island Gems

THESE DECADENT BARS always sell out at our library bake sale. The brown-sugar cookie crust is rich and buttery. It is topped with crunchy coconut, macadamia nuts and chocolate chips.

Cookie Layer

- ½ cup (1 stick) unsalted butter, softened
- ½ cup packed light brown sugar
- 1 teaspoon vanilla extract
- 1½ cups unbleached all-purpose flour

Coconut Layer

- 1 cup packed light brown sugar
- ¼ cup unbleached all-purpose flour
- ¼ teaspoon salt
- 1 teaspoon vanilla extract
- 2 large eggs
- 1 cup chopped macadamia nuts
- 1 3½-ounce can flaked sweetened coconut
- 1 cup semisweet chocolate chips

1. Preheat the oven to 350 degrees F. Lightly butter a 13-x-9-inch baking pan.
2. **To make the Cookie Layer:** In a large bowl, cream the butter, brown sugar and vanilla

with an electric mixer until light. Add the flour and beat just until blended. With floured fingertips, press the cookie dough into an even layer in the prepared pan. Bake for about 10 minutes, or until the edges are lightly browned. Cool on a wire rack. Leave the oven on.

3. **To make the Coconut Layer:** In a large bowl, beat the brown sugar, flour, salt, vanilla and eggs with an electric mixer until smooth. Stir in the macadamia nuts and the coconut. Spread over the cooled cookie layer. Sprinkle the top evenly with the chocolate chips.

4. Bake for 20 to 25 minutes, or until the edges are golden brown. Cool thoroughly before cutting into bars with a small sturdy knife.

MAKES 24 BARS

Jam Bars

T HESE BARS ARE very pretty and fun to make. You can use any jam, but I love them with orange marmalade. Be creative when you cut the bar shapes so that each one shows off a strip or two of your handy pastry "lattice" work.

2½ cups unbleached all-purpose flour

2 cups sugar

1 teaspoon grated orange zest

½ teaspoon salt

¾ cup (1½ sticks) cold unsalted butter, cut into small pieces

2 large eggs

1 teaspoon vanilla extract

1 cup jam (apricot, strawberry, raspberry, cherry or marmalade)

Confectioners' sugar

1. Lightly butter a 13-x-9-inch baking pan.

2. Combine the flour, sugar, orange zest and salt in the bowl of a food processor. With the motor running, add the butter, a few pieces at a time, until the mixture is crumbly.

3. Beat the eggs and vanilla until blended. With the processor running, add the eggs in a steady stream. Process until the mixture forms a dough. Turn out on a lightly floured surface and shape into a disc. Cut in half.

4. Roll out half of the dough between 2 sheets of wax paper into a 13-x-9-inch rectangle. Lift off the top sheet of wax paper and invert the dough over the prepared baking pan. Peel off the remaining wax paper. If the dough tears, simply press it together with your fingertips. Using a small paring knife, trim the dough to cover the bottom of the pan evenly. Refrigerate until ready to bake. Add the trimmings to the remaining dough.

5. Roll out the remaining dough between 2 sheets of wax paper to a strip at least 13 inches long and at least 5 inches wide. Slide the dough onto a baking sheet and freeze for about 20 minutes, or until the dough is very cold.

6. Preheat the oven to 350 degrees F.

7. Just before assembling, remove the pan with the bottom crust from the refrigerator and spread it with a thin layer of the jam. Remove the pastry from the freezer; lift off the top sheet of wax paper. Cut the dough into 9 strips, each about ½ inch wide. Peel the strips off

the bottom layer of wax paper, one at a time, and carefully arrange 5 strips lengthwise over the jam, spacing them evenly; trim the ends to fit. Cut the remaining strips into 9-inch lengths and arrange them evenly crosswise over the lengthwise strips; trim the ends.

8. Bake for 25 to 30 minutes, or until the edges are golden. Cool on a wire rack. Place the confectioners' sugar in a small strainer and sprinkle it evenly over the surface. Cut into bars.

MAKES ABOUT 24 BARS

Kahlúa Cheesecake Bars

THE CHOCOLATE BROWNIE-LIKE layer that forms the base of this bar cookie is spiked with a little powdered instant espresso coffee. The top layer is a thick cheesecake, fashioned after my favorite recipe, laced with Kahlúa. (You can substitute any coffee liqueur.)

Brownie Layer

- 6 tablespoons (¾ stick) unsalted butter
- 6 1-ounce squares semisweet chocolate
- ¾ cup unbleached all-purpose flour
- ½ teaspoon baking powder
- ¼ teaspoon salt
- ¾ cup packed light brown sugar
- 2 large eggs
- 1 tablespoon powdered instant espresso coffee
- 1 teaspoon vanilla extract

Cheesecake Layer

- 1 8-ounce package cream cheese, softened
- ½ cup sugar
- 2 tablespoons unbleached all-purpose flour
- 2 large eggs
- 3 tablespoons Kahlúa
- 1 teaspoon vanilla extract
- ½ teaspoon ground cinnamon

Sour Cream Layer

- 1½ cups sour cream
- ⅓ cup sugar

1. Preheat the oven to 350 degrees F. Lightly butter a 13-x-9-inch baking pan.

2. **To make the Brownie Layer:** In a small saucepan, melt the butter and chocolate over low heat. (Or place them in a heatproof bowl and microwave on high, stirring every 30 seconds, until melted, about 2 minutes.) Set aside to cool.

3. Sift together the flour, baking powder and salt; set aside. In a large bowl, beat the brown sugar, eggs, powdered coffee and vanilla until blended. Stir in the cooled chocolate mixture; add the flour mixture; stir until blended. Spread the batter into an even layer in the prepared pan.

4. **To make the Cheesecake Layer:** In a large bowl, beat the cream cheese, sugar and flour with an electric mixer until light and fluffy. Add the eggs, one at a time, beating well after each addition. Beat in the Kahlúa, vanilla and cinnamon until blended. Carefully pour over the brownie layer and spread into an even layer. Bake for 20 minutes, or until the top is almost set.

5. Meanwhile, **make the Sour Cream Layer**: Stir together the sour cream and sugar. After the bars have baked for 20 minutes, remove the pan from the oven and carefully spread the sour cream mixture over the top. Return to the oven and bake for 10 minutes. Cool thoroughly on a wire rack for several hours before cutting into bars.

6. To cut into bars, use a moistened knife and rinse and wipe the crumbs from the blade often while cutting. Refrigerate the bars if your kitchen is warm, but the flavor is best when the bars are eaten at room temperature.

MAKES 24 BARS

Keep-Forever Lizzies

WHEN I FIRST MET "Lizzie," she was a fruitcake-like cookie, filled with candied red and green cherries, pineapple and orange peel. Over the years, Lizzie became more modern in taste, as the candied fruits were slowly replaced by more natural ingredients, like dried figs, apricots, raisins and apples. Today the new, made-over Lizzie is a moist and chewy bar. For a special kick, I soak the raisins overnight in brandy or another spirit.

1   cup dark raisins
⅓   cup brandy, rum or bourbon
2   cups coarsely chopped walnuts, pecans or unsalted roasted cashews
½   cup snipped (½-inch pieces) dried apricots
½   cup snipped (½-inch pieces) pitted prunes
½   cup snipped (½-inch pieces) Calimyrna figs, stems trimmed
½   cup golden raisins

½   cup snipped (½-inch pieces) dried apples
½   cup (1 stick) unsalted butter, softened
1   cup packed light brown sugar
2   large eggs
1   teaspoon vanilla extract
1½ cups unbleached all-purpose flour
1   teaspoon baking powder
1   teaspoon ground cinnamon
¼   teaspoon freshly grated nutmeg
    About 1 cup confectioners' sugar

1. Combine the raisins and the brandy, rum or bourbon in a small bowl; toss to coat. Cover and let stand overnight, stirring occasionally. (To quick-soak the raisins, heat them in the liquor and let stand until cool.) Set aside.

2. Preheat the oven to 350 degrees F. Lightly butter a 13-x-9-inch baking pan.

3. Combine the walnuts, pecans or cashews and all of the dried fruits in a bowl; set aside. In a large bowl, beat together the butter and brown

sugar with an electric mixer until light. Add the eggs, one at a time, beating well after each addition, and add the vanilla. Sift together the flour, baking powder, cinnamon and nutmeg. Add 2 tablespoons of the flour mixture to the dried fruits; toss to coat. Add the remaining flour mixture to the butter mix-ture and beat until blended. Add the dried fruits and the soaked raisins to the batter and stir to blend.

4. Spread the batter in the prepared pan. Bake for about 25 minutes, or until the edges begin to pull away from the sides of the pan. Cool thoroughly on a wire rack before cutting into bars.

5. Spoon the confectioners' sugar onto a plate. Roll the bars in the sugar to coat; shake off the excess; wrap individually in plastic wrap. These are especially good keepers.

MAKES 24 BARS

Lemon Curd Bars

S OME OF US YEARN for chocolate and lemon combined. Here we have it: a crisp sugar-cookie base, a thin chocolate-candy layer and a soft lemon-curd-like topping. Not too sweet, very sophisticated and yummy.

Crust

1¾ cups unbleached all-purpose flour

½ cup confectioners' sugar

¼ teaspoon salt

1 cup (2 sticks) cold unsalted butter, cut into small pieces

1 teaspoon vanilla extract

4 1-ounce squares semisweet chocolate, coarsely chopped

Lemon Curd Layer

4 large eggs

2 cups sugar

⅓ cup unbleached all-purpose flour

2 teaspoons grated lemon zest

¾ cup fresh lemon juice

Confectioners' sugar

1. Preheat the oven to 350 degrees F. Generously butter a 13-x-9-inch baking pan.

2. **To make the Crust:** Combine the flour, confectioners' sugar and salt in a food processor. Process to blend. With the motor running, quickly add the pieces of butter through the feed tube. Add the vanilla. Process just until the mixture comes together in a ball.

3. With floured fingers, press the dough into an even layer in the prepared pan. Bake on the center rack for about 20 minutes, or until the edges are golden. Cool on a wire rack.

4. Meanwhile, melt the chocolate over low heat in a small heavy saucepan. Spread in an even layer over the cookie crust. Refrigerate until the chocolate is solid, about 20 minutes.

5. **To make the Lemon Curd Layer:** In a large bowl, beat or whisk the eggs until well blended. In a separate bowl, stir together the sugar, flour and lemon zest until blended. Gently beat or whisk the sugar mixture into the eggs just until blended. Gradually stir in the lemon juice until blended. Immediately pour over the chocolate and cookie layer.

6. Bake the bars for 25 to 30 minutes, or until the top is set. Cool thoroughly on a wire rack. Sprinkle with confectioners' sugar before cutting into bars.

MAKES 24 BARS

Lemon Love Notes

THESE ARE HEAVENLY: thin, crisp bars with a delicate taste of lemon and coconut, a tangy lemon glaze and a sprinkling of coconut on top.

Batter

1¾ cups unbleached all-purpose flour

½ teaspoon salt

1 cup (2 sticks) unsalted butter, softened

1 cup confectioners' sugar, sifted

1 large egg

1 cup flaked sweetened coconut

1 tablespoon grated lemon zest

Glaze

2 cups sifted confectioners' sugar

¼ cup fresh lemon juice

⅓ cup flaked sweetened coconut

1. Preheat the oven to 350 degrees F. Lightly butter a 13-x-9-inch baking pan.

2. **To make the Batter:** Sift the flour and salt together; set aside. In a large bowl, cream together the butter and confectioners' sugar with an electric mixer until light and fluffy. Beat in the egg until blended. Gradually add the flour mixture until blended; stir in the coconut and lemon zest.

3. Spread the batter in the prepared pan. Bake on the center rack for 20 to 25 minutes, or until the edges just begin to pull away from the sides of the pan. Do not overbake. Cool on a wire rack. Glaze the bars while still warm.

4. **To make the Glaze:** In a bowl, stir together the confectioners' sugar and lemon juice until smooth. Drizzle the mixture over the warm cookies, and spread evenly with a small flexible spatula. Sprinkle with the coconut. Cool thoroughly before cutting into bars.

MAKES 24 BARS

Meringue Bars

THIS RECIPE USES almonds in two ways: ground in the cookie crust and thinly sliced in the meringue layer. The bars are light, slightly chewy and not overly sweet. You can also spread a thin layer of strawberry jam on the crust before adding the almond meringue. Sliced, slivered or whole almonds can be used for the cookie layer since they will be finely ground. For the meringue, use the thin-sliced almonds; either blanched or unblanched (with skins) are fine.

Crust

- ⅓ cup sliced, slivered or whole almonds
- 1 cup unbleached all-purpose flour
- ⅓ cup sugar
- ½ cup (1 stick) cold unsalted butter, cut into small pieces

Topping

- 1½ cups sliced natural (unblanched) or blanched almonds
- 3 large egg whites, at room temperature
- ¼ cup sugar
- ½ teaspoon almond extract

Confectioners' sugar

66

1. Preheat the oven to 350 degrees F. Lightly butter a 13-x-9-inch baking pan.

2. **To make the Crust:** Finely grind the almonds in a food processor. Add the flour and sugar; process to blend. With the motor running, add the butter, a few pieces at a time, until the mixture is crumbly. Sprinkle evenly over the bottom of the prepared pan and press the crumbs into an even layer.

3. Bake the cookie crust for 8 to 10 minutes, or just until the edges begin to turn golden. Cool on a wire rack. Leave the oven on.

4. **To make the Topping:** Spread the almonds on a baking sheet and toast just until golden, about 8 minutes. Cool before using. Leave the oven on.

5. In a large bowl, beat the egg whites with an electric mixer until soft peaks form. Gradually add the sugar and beat until the whites are stiff and shiny. Stir in the almond extract. Fold in 1 cup of the toasted almonds. Spread the meringue in an even layer over the cookie crust. Sprinkle the top with the remaining ½ cup toasted almonds.

6. Bake the bars for about 25 minutes, or until the meringue is evenly golden brown. Cool on a wire rack. Sprinkle with confectioners' sugar before carefully cutting into bars with a sturdy knife.

MAKES 24 BARS

Mammy's Chocolate Chip Bars

S ENSIBLE, HOMEY, nothing fussy. Chances are you already have all these ingredients—flour, sugar, shortening, eggs, walnuts and chocolate chips—on hand. This old-fashioned recipe is from my husband's grandmother. The Simmons family owned a dairy farm in northwestern New Jersey where Pappy took care of business in the barn and Mammy took care of the kitchen. These bars have been a favorite treat for four generations of Simmons children.

2¾ cups unbleached all-purpose flour

2½ teaspoons baking powder

½ teaspoon salt

⅔ cup solid vegetable shortening, melted

2¼ cups packed (1-pound box) light brown sugar

3 large eggs, beaten

1 cup coarsely chopped walnuts

1½ cups semisweet chocolate chips

1. Preheat the oven to 350 degrees F. Lightly butter a 13-x-9-inch baking pan.

2. Sift together the flour, baking powder and salt; set aside.

3. In a large bowl, combine the shortening and brown sugar. Beat the eggs together in a small bowl and gradually add them to the sugar mixture. Stir with a wooden spoon until the mixture is smooth and lighter in color.

4. Gradually stir in the dry ingredients until blended; the mixture will be very stiff. Add the walnuts and chocolate chips; stir to blend.

5. Spread the batter in the prepared pan and smooth with a spatula. Bake for 25 to 30 minutes, or until the edges begin to pull away from the sides of the pan. Cool on a wire rack before cutting into bars.

MAKES 24 BARS

Marmalade Brownies

DENSE, DARK and more a confection than a cake or cookie, these brownies have elicited two marriage proposals and one request for adoption. For sophisticated balance and taste, use a bitter orange marmalade and a good-quality chocolate.

⅓ cup (5⅓ tablespoons) unsalted butter	½ teaspoon vanilla extract
2 1-ounce squares unsweetened chocolate	⅔ cup unbleached all-purpose flour
½ cup packed light brown sugar	½ cup chopped walnuts
½ cup orange marmalade	Pinch of salt
2 large eggs, beaten	

1. Preheat the oven to 350 degrees F. Butter or oil a 9-inch square baking pan.

2. Place the butter and chocolate in a medium nonaluminum saucepan and heat over low heat until melted. Remove from the heat. Add the brown sugar and marmalade; beat with a wooden spoon until blended.

3. Add the eggs and vanilla and stir until blended. Add the flour, walnuts and salt; stir to blend.

4. Spread the batter in the prepared pan. Bake for 25 minutes, or until the edges begin to pull away from the sides of the pan. Cool slightly on a wire rack before cutting into bars.

MAKES 18 BARS

Nutter Doodles

"**P**ASS THOSE nutter doodles things . . . please," chirped a little voice from the end of the table. Now, thanks to my niece, these yummy bars have a distinctive name. These are cakelike but chewy, with toasted pieces of chopped pecans and lots of chocolate chips, like a cube-shaped chocolate chip cookie, or a blondie with specks of chocolate. I like the flavor of pecans, especially when toasted, but toasted walnuts will do, if you prefer.

1½ **cups pecan halves**	1 **cup packed light brown sugar**
2 **cups unbleached all-purpose flour**	2 **large eggs, lightly beaten**
1 **teaspoon baking powder**	2 **teaspoons vanilla extract**
½ **teaspoon salt**	1 **cup semisweet chocolate chips**
1 **cup (2 sticks) unsalted butter, softened**	

1. Preheat the oven to 350 degrees F. Lightly butter a 13-x-9-inch baking pan.

2. Spread the pecans on a baking sheet and bake for 10 minutes, or until lightly toasted; set aside to cool. Leave the oven on.

3. Sift together the flour, baking powder and salt; set aside. In a large bowl, cream the butter and brown sugar with an electric mixer until light and fluffy. Add the eggs and

vanilla; beat until blended. Add the sifted dry ingredients and beat just until blended. Stir in the chocolate chips and 1 cup of the toasted pecans.

4. Spread the batter in the prepared pan; sprinkle the top with the remaining ½ cup pecans. Bake on the center rack for 20 to 25 minutes, or until the edges begin to pull away from the sides of the pan. Cool on a wire rack before cutting into bars.

MAKES 24 BARS

Nutmeg Bars

THIS RECIPE MAKES a big batch of thin, crisp bars, heady with the aroma of nutmeg and crunchy with toasted hazelnuts (also called filberts). Freeze them in flat foil packets of 10 or 12 and keep on hand for a last-minute sweet to serve with after-dinner coffee. They are also good when made with walnuts or pecans. If you don't care for the taste of nutmeg, try them with cinnamon.

1 cup hazelnuts (filberts)	1 large egg, separated
1 cup (2 sticks) unsalted butter, softened	1¾ cups unbleached all-purpose flour
1 cup packed light brown sugar	1 teaspoon freshly grated nutmeg
1 teaspoon vanilla extract	½ teaspoon salt

1. Preheat the oven to 350 degrees F. Spread the hazelnuts in a small baking pan. Bake until the skins crack and the nuts are lightly browned, about 10 to 15 minutes. Leave the oven on.

2. Transfer the nuts to a large dish towel and rub vigorously to remove the skins. Separate the nuts from the skins. Finely chop the nuts in a food processor; separate into 2 portions, ½ cup each.

3. Meanwhile, lightly butter a 15-x-10-x-1-inch baking pan; set aside.

4. In a large bowl, beat the butter, brown sugar, vanilla and egg yolk with an electric mixer until light. In a separate bowl, stir together the flour, nutmeg and salt. Add the dry ingredients to the butter mixture, along with ½ cup of the nuts. Stir until well blended. Spread the batter into the prepared pan and smooth with a small spatula.

5. Lightly beat the egg white with a fork. Brush the surface of the batter with a thin film of the egg white. Evenly sprinkle on the remaining ½ cup nuts. Press the nuts down lightly with your fingers so they will stick to the dough.

6. Bake for 25 minutes, or until lightly browned. Cool slightly on a wire rack, but cut into bars while they are still warm. Cool thoroughly before removing from the pan. The bars will become crisp.

MAKES **28** BARS

Orange & Cranberry Ginger-Oat Bars

THESE BARS ARE PERFECT for the "too-sweet-for-me" set. The orange-cranberry filling is quite tangy, and the oatmeal crust and topping lend a natural sweetness and pleasant cakelike texture.

Filling

1	12-ounce package whole cranberries, fresh or frozen, rinsed and picked over
¾	cup water
¾	cup sugar
1	tablespoon grated fresh ginger
1	tablespoon grated orange zest

Crust & Topping

1¾	cups unbleached all-purpose flour
2	teaspoons ground ginger
1	teaspoon baking powder
½	teaspoon salt
1	cup (2 sticks) unsalted butter, softened
1	cup packed light brown sugar
2	large eggs
1½	cups old-fashioned oatmeal

1. **To make the Filling:** In a medium nonaluminum saucepan, heat the cranberries, water, sugar, ginger and orange zest until boiling; cook over medium heat until all of the cranberries "pop" and the mixture is thickened, about 10 minutes. Remove from the heat. Transfer to a shallow plate or bowl and refrigerate until cooled and very thick. (The filling can be made up to 1 day ahead.)

2. Preheat the oven to 350 degrees F. Lightly butter a 13-x-9-inch baking pan.

3. **To make the Crust and Topping:** Sift together the flour, ginger, baking powder and salt; set aside. In a large bowl, beat the butter and brown sugar with an electric mixer until light and fluffy. Add the eggs, one at a time, beating well after each addition. Beat in the sifted mixture and the oatmeal just until blended.

4. Reserve about 1½ cups of the dough for the topping. Spread the remaining dough in an even layer in the prepared baking pan. Spoon the cranberry filling over the dough and spread in an even layer. Using floured fingertips, sprinkle small clumps of the reserved dough over the cranberries.

5. Bake for 35 to 40 minutes, or until the edges and top are golden brown. Cool on a wire rack before cutting into bars.

MAKES 24 BARS

Old-Fashioned Oatmeal & Raisin Bars

Tasting exactly like oatmeal cookies, these bars are easier to make because they can be baked in one pan instead of fiddling with spoonfuls of batter on baking sheets.

1	**cup unbleached all-purpose flour**
1	**teaspoon ground cinnamon**
½	**teaspoon baking powder**
	Pinch of salt
¾	**cup (1½ sticks) unsalted butter, softened**
¾	**cup packed light brown sugar**
1	**large egg**
1	**teaspoon vanilla extract**
2	**cups old-fashioned oatmeal**
1	**cup dark raisins**

1. Preheat the oven to 350 degrees F. Lightly butter a 13-x-9-inch baking pan.

2. Sift together the flour, cinnamon, baking powder and salt; set aside. In a large bowl, beat the butter and brown sugar with an electric mixer until light and fluffy. Beat in the egg and vanilla. Add the dry ingredients; beat until blended. Fold in the oatmeal and raisins with a wooden spoon until well blended.

3. Spread the batter in the prepared pan. Bake for 25 to 30 minutes, or until the edges begin to pull away from the sides of the pan. Cool on a wire rack before cutting into bars.

MAKES 24 BARS

Pignoli Bars

To CREATE THESE BARS, I folded toasted pine nuts into a recipe for frangipane filling (eggs, sugar and ground almonds) from Paula Peck's classic book, *The Art of Fine Baking*. Ms. Peck, whom I never met (she is now deceased), taught me to bake through her wonderful collection of recipes. I like to think that she would approve of these chewy, sophisticated bars.

Crust

½   **cup (1 stick) cold unsalted butter, cut into small pieces**

½   **cup packed light brown sugar**

1¼ **cups unbleached all-purpose flour**

1   **cup pignoli (pine nuts)**

Topping

½   **cup (1 stick) unsalted butter, softened**

2   **large eggs**

7-8 **ounces almond paste, cut into small pieces**

1   **tablespoon unbleached all-purpose flour**

1   **teaspoon grated lemon zest**

¼   **cup apricot preserves or jam**

1. Preheat the oven to 350 degrees F. Lightly butter a 13-x-9-inch baking pan.

2. **To make the Crust:** In a large bowl, cream the butter and brown sugar with an electric mixer until light. Add the flour and beat just until blended and crumbly. Sprinkle the mixture evenly over the bottom of the prepared pan. Press into an even layer. Bake for about 8 minutes, or until golden. Cool on a wire rack. Leave the oven on.

3. Meanwhile, place the pignoli in a dry medium-sized skillet. Turn the heat to medium-low and toast, stirring constantly, until the nuts begin to turn golden, about 3 minutes. Do not leave them unattended; they burn very quickly. Remove from the pan; set aside to cool.

4. **To make the Topping:** In a large bowl, cream the butter with an electric mixer. Whisk the eggs in a small bowl. Gradually add the bits of almond paste alternately with the beaten eggs to the butter; beat until light and fluffy. Beat in the flour and lemon zest.

5. Coarsely chop half of the toasted pignoli; fold into the topping. Spread the topping over the prebaked crust. Bake for 20 to 25 minutes, or until the topping is golden. Cool on a wire rack.

6. Heat the apricot preserves in a small saucepan until melted, or microwave for about 1 minute. Strain through a small sieve. Brush the warm strained preserves over the bars. Sprinkle the remaining ½ cup toasted pignoli evenly over the top. Cut into bars.

MAKES 24 BARS

Peanut Butter-Chocolate Bars

T HE DAY YOU BAKE THEM, these bars have the dry texture of a peanut butter cookie, but by the next day they are more like candy: dense, peanuty and solid. They are a real treat for peanut-butter-and-chocolate fans.

Batter

2¼ cups unbleached all-purpose flour

1 teaspoon baking powder

Pinch of salt

1 cup (2 sticks) unsalted butter, softened

1½ cups packed light brown sugar

1 cup creamy peanut butter

1 teaspoon vanilla extract

2 large eggs

1 cup coarsely chopped dry-roasted unsalted peanuts

Topping

6 1-ounce squares semisweet chocolate

½ cup heavy cream

1. Preheat the oven to 350 degrees F. Lightly butter a 13-x-9-inch baking pan.

2. **To make the Batter:** Sift together the flour, baking powder and salt onto a sheet of wax paper; set aside. In a large bowl, cream the butter and brown sugar with an electric mixer until light. Beat in the peanut butter and vanilla until blended. Add the eggs, one at a time, beating well after each addition. Gradually beat in the flour mixture until blended. Fold in the peanuts.

3. Spread the batter in the prepared pan. Bake for 25 to 30 minutes, or until the edges begin to pull away from the sides of the pan. Cool thoroughly on a wire rack.

4. **To make the Topping:** Combine the chocolate and heavy cream in a small saucepan. Heat over low heat, stirring gently, until the chocolate is almost completely melted. (Or place the chocolate and heavy cream in a heatproof bowl and microwave on high, stirring every 30 seconds, until melted.) Remove from the heat and stir until smooth. Cool slightly. Spread the chocolate in an even layer over the cooled bars. Let stand until set. Cut into bars.

MAKES 24 BARS

Prune & Molasses Crumb Bars

J UST IN CASE you are watching your cholesterol, these happen to be eggless and butter-less. The combination of molasses and prunes gives these bars a sumptuous taste.

Filling

1½ cups pitted prunes, snipped into small
     (½-inch) pieces with scissors
¾   cup water
1   teaspoon grated lemon zest
1   tablespoon fresh lemon juice

Crumbs

½   cup minus 1 tablespoon vegetable oil
⅓   cup unsulphured molasses
½   cup packed light brown sugar
1   cup unbleached all-purpose flour
½   cup whole-wheat flour
1   teaspoon ground cinnamon
    Pinch of salt
½   cup finely chopped walnuts

1. Preheat the oven to 350 degrees F. Lightly butter a 9-inch square baking pan.

2. **To make the Filling:** Combine the prunes, water and lemon zest in a medium non-aluminum saucepan. Cook, covered, over low heat until the moisture is absorbed and the prunes are very tender, about 10 minutes. Uncover and stir in the lemon juice. Set aside to cool.

3. **To make the Crumbs:** In a medium bowl, combine the vegetable oil, molasses and brown sugar; whisk to blend. Add the flours, cinnamon, salt and walnuts. Stir to blend, first using a spoon and then your hands, until the mixture is very crumbly. Reserve 1 cup of the crumbs for the topping.

4. Sprinkle the remaining crumbs over the bottom of the prepared pan and press into an even layer. Spoon the prune filling evenly over the bottom crust; spread into a thin layer with a small flexible spatula. Sprinkle the reserved crumbs evenly over the top.

5. Bake for 25 minutes, or until the edges begin to pull away from the sides of the pan. Cool on a wire rack before cutting into bars.

MAKES 18 BARS

Pumpkin & Walnut Praline Bars

T HESE BARS ARE LIKE delicate rectangles of classic pumpkin pie. The bottom dough is a basic pie crust, while the pumpkin layer is topped with a crunchy praline mixture of brown sugar, butter and walnuts.

Crust

1½	cups all-purpose unbleached flour
1	tablespoon sugar
	Pinch of salt
½	cup solid vegetable shortening
3-4	tablespoons ice water
1	large egg white, lightly beaten

Filling

1	cup canned solid-packed pumpkin
3	large eggs
⅔	cup packed light brown sugar
1	teaspoon ground cinnamon
¼	teaspoon freshly grated nutmeg
¾	cup evaporated milk

Topping

½	cup packed light brown sugar
1	tablespoon unbleached all-purpose flour
2	tablespoons unsalted butter, softened
1	cup chopped walnuts

1. Preheat the oven to 350 degrees F. Lightly butter a 13-x-9-inch baking pan.

2. **To make the Crust:** In a large bowl, stir together the flour, sugar and salt. Cut in the shortening with a pastry blender or 2 knives until the mixture is the consistency of rough cornmeal. Add the ice water gradually, while stirring lightly with a fork, just until the dough begins to form a ball. Gather the dough together with floured hands.

3. Cut a 13-x-9-inch piece of wax paper or foil and place it on a flat surface. Place the dough in the center and roll with a lightly floured rolling pin to fit the paper as perfectly as possible. Lifting the dough by the paper, invert it into the prepared pan. Lift off and discard the paper. Trim the edges of the dough to fit the pan. Brush lightly with a little of the beaten egg white and refrigerate until ready to bake.

4. **To make the Filling:** In a large bowl, combine the pumpkin, eggs, brown sugar, cinnamon and nutmeg; whisk until smooth. Gradually stir in the evaporated milk until blended.

5. Pour the filling over the crust in the prepared pan. Bake for 25 minutes. Remove from the oven and let stand for 5 minutes. Leave the oven on.

6. Meanwhile, **make the Topping:** Blend together the brown sugar and flour in a bowl; add the butter and blend with your fingertips or a fork until mixed and crumbly. Add the walnuts and stir to blend. Sprinkle the topping evenly over the surface of the pumpkin filling. Return the bars to the oven and bake for about 15 minutes, or until lightly browned. Cool on a wire rack before cutting into bars.

MAKES 24 BARS

Queen Victoria Dream Bars

T HIS FLAT, BUTTERY AND TENDER bar cookie has a multilayered orange flavor. First comes the light, fresh taste of orange zest and juice, and then the sweet tang of candied peel. If possible, buy the orange peel in bulk at a specialty store. It is much better-tasting than the overly sugared candied rinds found in many supermarkets. I prefer these not-too-sweet, regal, cakelike cookies with a cup of tea.

½   **cup (1 stick) unsalted butter, softened**
1   **cup confectioners' sugar, plus more for sprinkling over bars**
1   **large egg**
3   **tablespoons fresh orange juice**

1½   **cups unbleached all-purpose flour**
½   **teaspoon baking powder**
2   **teaspoons grated orange zest**
½   **cup chopped candied orange peel**

1. Preheat the oven to 350 degrees F. Lightly butter an 11-x-7-inch or 9-inch square baking pan.

2. In a large bowl, cream the butter and sugar with an electric mixer until light and fluffy. Beat in the egg until blended. Gradually add the orange juice until blended. (The mixture will look curdled.)

3. In a separate bowl, sift together the flour and baking powder. Add the grated orange zest and candied orange peel. Stir to coat. Add the flour mixture to the butter mixture; stir to blend.

4. Spread the batter into the prepared pan. Bake for 20 to 25 minutes, or until the edges are golden. Cool on a wire rack. Sprinkle with a layer of sieved confectioners' sugar before cutting into bars.

MAKES 18 BARS

Quaresimale Bars

REMINISCENT OF BISCOTTI, this recipe was inspired by Richard Sax, a good friend, collaborator and expert baker. Richard explains that his recipe was derived from one given to him by Joe Fighera, a baker at Veniero Bakery in New York City, who taught him that quaresimale should be hard "like glass." The name derives from the Italian *quaresima*, which means Lent, the time at which these biscuits are traditionally eaten. This simplified version is quite hard and crunchy—great dipped into caffé latte or espresso.

2 cups whole natural (unblanched) almonds, coarsely chopped	1 teaspoon baking powder
1½ cups unbleached all-purpose flour	¼ teaspoon salt
½ cup packed light brown sugar	⅓ cup olive oil
¼ cup sugar	2 large eggs
1 teaspoon ground cinnamon	¼ teaspoon almond extract

1. Preheat the oven to 350 degrees F. Line a 13-x-9-inch baking pan with a piece of foil long enough to cover the bottom and the long sides of the pan. Tuck under any excess foil. Lightly butter the foil and the short sides of the pan.

2. In a large bowl, combine the almonds, flour, sugars, cinnamon, baking powder and salt; stir to blend.

3. In a small bowl, whisk together the oil, eggs and almond extract. Add the oil mixture to the dry ingredients. Stir with a wooden spoon until blended and the mixture looks moist but is still crumbly.

4. Spread the mixture evenly in the prepared pan and press down with floured fingertips. Bake for 20 minutes.

5. Remove from the oven and score the top of the dough into 24 bar cookies. Return to the oven and bake for about 20 minutes more, or until the edges are browned.

6. Cool the bars on a wire rack before lifting from the pan, using the long edges of the foil. Break into bars along the score marks.

MAKES 24 BARS

Raspberry & Hazelnut Shortbread Bars

INZER TARTS —two round discs filled with raspberry jam —have always been my favorites. I have adapted the idea to a cookie. These melt-in-your-mouth, jam-filled bars are very good. The cookie layers are soft but chewy, almost cakelike. Make sure to use a good-quality raspberry jam. These are best after they have mellowed for one day.

⅔　cup hazelnuts (filberts)

1½　cups unbleached all-purpose flour

½　cup sugar

1　teaspoon baking powder

1　teaspoon ground cinnamon

1　teaspoon grated lemon zest

½　teaspoon salt

½　cup cold unsalted butter, cut into small pieces

2　large eggs

½　teaspoon vanilla extract

1　cup raspberry jam

　　Confectioners' sugar

1. Preheat the oven to 350 degrees F. Lightly butter a 9-inch square baking pan.

2. Spread the hazelnuts on a baking sheet and bake until the skins crack and the nuts are lightly toasted, 10 to 15 minutes. Turn the nuts into a large dish towel and rub vigorously to remove the loosened skins. Separate the nuts from the skins. Leave the oven on.

3. Grind the nuts in a food processor until quite fine. Remove 2 tablespoons and set aside. Add the flour, sugar, baking powder, cinnamon, lemon zest and salt and process to blend. With the motor running, gradually add the butter; process just until blended.

4. In a small bowl, whisk the eggs with the vanilla. Gradually add the egg mixture to the processor, pulsing on and off just until the mixture forms a dough; do not overprocess or the dough will be too sticky.

5. Divide the dough in half. Working between 2 sheets of wax paper, roll out half of the dough into an 11-inch circle. Slide the dough onto a baking sheet and freeze for 15 minutes. Press the remaining dough into the bottom of the prepared pan; refrigerate until the top crust is ready.

6. Spread the chilled bottom crust with the raspberry jam. Remove the baking sheet from the freezer; peel off the top layer of wax paper. Cut the dough into a perfect 9-inch square using a ruler or the pan as a guide. Invert the top crust onto the jam-spread bottom crust in the pan. Remove the remaining sheet of wax paper. Lightly sprinkle with the reserved hazelnuts.

7. Bake for 25 to 30 minutes, or until the top is golden brown. Cool on a wire rack. Using a small strainer, sprinkle evenly with a layer of confectioners' sugar. Let stand for at least 3 hours before cutting into bars.

MAKES 18 BARS

Rice Krispie-Sesame Bars

A GOOD FRIEND AND WONDERFUL COOK, Dalia Carmel Goldstein, who was born in Israel, remembers these no-bake bars from her childhood. Made with rice cereal, melted halvah (a finely ground sesame-seed candy) and honey, it's similar to the American cereal-box favorite made from rice cereal and melted marshmallows. Halvah, sold in small candy-bar portions and by the ounce from a large chunk, is available in many delis, Middle Eastern stores and specialty-food shops.

1 cup sesame seeds	2 tablespoons honey
6-8 ounces plain (vanilla) halvah, cut into small pieces	5 cups rice cereal (such as Rice Krispies)
6 tablespoons (¾ stick) unsalted butter, cut into small pieces	

1. Line a 13-x-9-inch baking pan with a piece of foil long enough to cover the bottom and the long sides of the pan. Tuck under any excess foil. Lightly oil the foil and the short sides of the pan.

2. In a dry medium-sized skillet, toast the sesame seeds, stirring constantly over low heat, for about 3 minutes. Do not leave unattended, because once the skillet gets hot, the sesame seeds can burn very quickly. Transfer to a glass measuring cup.

3. Place the halvah and the butter in the skillet and heat over medium heat, stirring occasionally, until melted, about 5 minutes. Stir in the honey.

4. Place the rice cereal in a large bowl. Add the melted halvah mixture and ¾ cup of the toasted sesame seeds; stir to blend. Quickly transfer the mixture to the prepared pan and use a rubber spatula to spread it into an even layer. Sprinkle the top evenly with the remaining ¼ cup sesame seeds.

5. Cut into large bars (5 across and 4 down) while still warm. Let cool completely before removing them from the pan. To remove, take the foil by the long ends and lift the bars from the baking pan. Peel off the foil and divide into bars.

MAKES 20 BARS

Sticky Pecan Bars

F ASHIONED AFTER our family's favorite pecan tart recipe, these bars are made of moist, chewy nuts set on an easy-to-make butter cookie dough.

Crust

1½ cups unbleached all-purpose flour

¼ cup sugar

Pinch of salt

10 tablespoons (1 stick plus 2 tablespoons) cold unsalted butter, cut into pieces

1 large egg yolk

Filling

½ cup packed light brown sugar

2 tablespoons unbleached all-purpose flour

¾ cup dark corn syrup

3 large eggs

1 teaspoon vanilla extract

2 cups large pecan halves

1. Preheat the oven to 400 degrees F. Lightly butter a 9-inch square pan.

2. **To make the Crust:** Combine the flour, sugar and salt in the bowl of a food processor. With the motor running, gradually add the butter through the feed tube; process until blended. Add the egg yolk and process until blended. Turn out into the prepared pan and gather the dough together. Flatten with your hand and press evenly into the bottom of the pan, forming a ¼-inch edge up the sides of the pan. Refrigerate until ready to bake.

3. **To make the Filling:** In a medium-sized bowl, stir the brown sugar and flour until blended. Add the corn syrup, eggs and vanilla; whisk until well blended. Spread the pecans in an even layer over the crust. Pour the filling over the top.

4. Bake for 10 minutes. Reduce the oven temperature to 350 degrees, and bake for 25 minutes, or until the filling is firm. Cool on a wire rack before cutting into bars.

MAKES 18 BARS

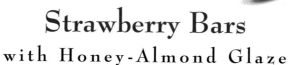

Strawberry Bars
with Honey-Almond Glaze

I**N THIS CHEWY BAR,** layers of cookie dough, strawberry jam or preserves, sliced almonds and honey glaze are all baked together.

¾ **cup strawberry jam or preserves**

Glaze

⅓ **cup (5⅓ tablespoons) unsalted butter**

¼ **cup sugar**

¼ **cup brandy**

2 **tablespoons honey**

Crust

1¾ **cups unbleached all-purpose flour**

½ **cup sugar**

¼ **teaspoon salt**

½ **cup unsalted butter, softened**

1 **large egg, beaten**

1 **cup sliced natural (unblanched) or blanched almonds**

1. Preheat the oven to 350 degrees F. Lightly butter a 15-x-10-x-1-inch baking pan.

2. Puree the strawberry jam or preserves in a food processor so it will spread evenly.

3. **To make the Glaze:** In a small saucepan, combine the butter, sugar, brandy and honey. Heat to boiling over low heat; boil 1 minute. Remove from the heat and set aside until ready to use.

4. **To make the Crust:** In a large bowl, stir together the flour, sugar and salt. With a pastry blender or 2 knives, cut in the butter until the pieces are very fine. Add the egg and blend with a fork until the mixture comes together. Using your hands, crumble the mixture evenly over the bottom of the pan. With floured fingertips, press the dough into an even layer.

5. Place the strawberry jam in a small saucepan and heat just until it is warmed and easy

to spread. Spread in a thin layer over the cookie dough. Sprinkle evenly with the sliced almonds. Drizzle with the honey glaze.

6. Bake the bars for 25 minutes, or until the edges are lightly browned. Cool thoroughly on a wire rack before cutting into bars.

MAKES **28** BARS

Sugar-Coated Date Temptations

As Oscar Wilde once said, "I can resist everything but temptation." He'd probably feel the same way about these dark, moist, chewy bars, dredged in confectioners' sugar.

1	8-ounce package chopped pitted dates	1	tablespoon vegetable oil
2	strips (½ x 2 inches) orange zest	1	tablespoon fresh lemon juice
6	tablespoons very hot water	½	cup unbleached all-purpose flour
2	cups confectioners' sugar	½	teaspoon ground cinnamon
2	large eggs, lightly beaten		Pinch of salt

1. Preheat the oven to 350 degrees F. Lightly butter a 9-inch square baking pan.

2. Finely chop the dates and orange zest in a food processor. With the motor running, gradually add the hot water to moisten the dates. Transfer to a large bowl.

3. Add 1 cup of the confectioners' sugar, the eggs, oil and lemon juice. Beat with a wooden spoon until blended. Add the flour, cinnamon and salt; stir until blended.

4. Spread the batter into the prepared pan. Bake for 25 minutes, or until the edges begin to pull away from the sides of the pan. Cool on a wire rack before cutting into bars.

5. Place the remaining 1 cup confectioners' sugar on a plate. Roll the bars in the sugar to coat them. These keep especially well.

MAKES 18 BARS

Susan's Frangipane Bars

FRANGIPANE, a rich mixture of ground almonds or almond paste, eggs and butter, is often used as a filling for small tarts. The following recipe, from a superb baker and my good friend Susan Westmoreland, builds a layered bar of pastry crust, cherry preserves and frangipane. They are perfect with an espresso or a cup of strong tea.

Crust

2¼ cups unbleached all-purpose flour

¼ cup sugar

⅛ teaspoon salt

½ cup (1 stick) cold unsalted butter, cut into small pieces

¼ cup solid vegetable shortening
   About ½ cup ice water

1 cup cherry preserves

Topping

1 cup sugar

7-8 ounces almond paste, cut into small pieces

½ cup (1 stick) unsalted butter, softened

4 large eggs

½ cup unbleached all-purpose flour

1 teaspoon vanilla extract

½ teaspoon almond extract

¼ teaspoon salt

1. Preheat the oven to 400 degrees F. Lightly butter a 15-x-10-x-1-inch baking pan.

2. **To make the Crust:** In a large bowl, combine the flour, sugar and salt. Add the butter and shortening and, using a pastry blender or 2 knives, cut in until the mixture resembles

coarse crumbs. Sprinkle with 1 tablespoon of the ice water at a time, and toss with a fork until the mixture begins to pull together as a dough. Gather into a ball and place on a lightly floured work surface.

3. Using a lightly floured rolling pin, roll out the dough into a rectangle large enough to cover the bottom and reach about one-fourth the way up the sides of the prepared pan (trim as needed). The crust will shrink slightly after it is prebaked. Fit the dough into the pan and press into place.

4. Bake the crust for about 15 minutes, or until lightly browned. Cool on a wire rack. Reduce the oven temperature to 350 degrees.

5. If the cherry preserves are especially lumpy, puree them briefly in a food processor until smooth. Spread into a thin layer over the cooled crust.

6. **To make the Topping:** In a large bowl, beat the sugar, almond paste and butter with an electric mixer until light and fluffy. Add the eggs, one at a time, beating well after each addition. Beat in the flour, the vanilla and almond extracts and salt until smooth. Spoon the topping over the cherry preserves, using a small spatula to spread it into an even layer.

7. Bake for about 30 minutes, or until lightly browned on top. (The frangipane will be browned on the edges and slightly soft in the center.) Cool thoroughly (the center will firm when cooled) on a wire rack before cutting into small bars, *7* across and *7* down.

MAKES 49 BARS

Toffee-Fudge Crunch Bars

T HESE EASY-TO-MAKE, impossible-to-resist chocolate toffee bars are made with Heath Bars that have been broken into small pieces. Already broken Heath Bits are available in 6-ounce bags in the candy section of supermarkets.

1 cup (2 sticks) unsalted butter, softened	¼ cup imported or European-style unsweetened cocoa powder
½ cup packed dark brown sugar	
1 teaspoon vanilla extract	½ teaspoon salt
2 cups unbleached all-purpose flour	2 cups coarsely crushed chocolate-coated toffee bars (Heath Bars)
⅓ cup cornstarch	

1. Preheat the oven to 350 degrees F. Lightly butter a 13-x-9-inch baking pan.

2. In a large bowl, cream the butter and brown sugar with an electric mixer. Stir in the vanilla until blended.

3. Sift together the flour, cornstarch, cocoa and salt. Stir the sifted ingredients into the butter mixture until blended. Add 1 cup of the crushed toffee bars; stir until blended.

4. Spread the batter into an even layer in the prepared pan. Sprinkle the remaining 1 cup crushed toffee bars on top and press in lightly with the back of a spoon.

5. Bake for 25 minutes, or until the edges begin to pull away from the sides of the pan. Cool on a wire rack before cutting into bars.

MAKES 24 BARS

Tropical Rain Forest Crunch Bars

T HANKS TO THE GENEROSITY of a favorite editor and publisher, I have become addicted to a candy called Tropical Rain Forest Crunch, which is like a peanut brittle, but made with cashews, brazil nuts and other exotic ingredients.

Caramel Brittle

½   cup (1 stick) unsalted butter

½   cup sugar

1   tablespoon water

1   tablespoon light corn syrup

Crust

½   cup (1 stick) unsalted butter, softened

½   cup packed light brown sugar

1   cup unbleached all-purpose flour

Topping

1   cup packed light brown sugar

2   large eggs

1   teaspoon vanilla extract

2   tablespoons unbleached all-purpose flour

1   teaspoon baking powder

½   teaspoon salt

1   cup shredded or flaked sweetened coconut

1   cup coarsely chopped toasted unsalted cashews

½   cup coarsely chopped shelled brazil nuts
    Confectioners' sugar

1. **To make the Caramel Brittle:** Lightly butter a large baking sheet; set aside. Melt the butter in a small, heavy saucepan over low heat. Stir in the sugar and cook, stirring, until dissolved. Add the water and corn syrup. Turn the heat to medium and boil the mixture. Cook, stirring occasionally, until the mixture turns golden and registers 290 degrees F on a candy thermometer, or hard-crack stage. (If you do not have a candy thermometer, test by dropping a small amount of the caramel mixture into a cup of ice water; it should turn hard and

brittle.) Pour the mixture onto the prepared baking pan. Cool completely, break into pieces; chop into smaller pieces. Measure out ½ cup. Store the remaining brittle for another use. (It's great on ice cream.) The brittle can be made several days ahead.

2. Preheat the oven to 350 degrees F. Lightly butter a 13-x-9-inch baking pan.

3. **To make the Crust:** In a large bowl, cream the butter and brown sugar with an electric mixer. Add the flour; beat just until the mixture is crumbly. Turn into the prepared pan and press the crumbs into an even layer over the bottom. Bake for about 8 minutes, or until golden. Cool. Leave the oven on.

4. **To make the Topping:** In a large bowl, beat the brown sugar, eggs and vanilla until blended. Add the flour, baking powder and salt; stir to blend. Add the coconut, cashews, brazil nuts and the ½ cup of caramel brittle; stir to blend. Spread the topping over the pre-baked crust.

5. Bake for about 25 minutes, or until golden brown. Cool thoroughly on a wire rack. Sprinkle lightly with confectioners' sugar before cutting into bars.

Makes 24 bars

Utterly Delicious Bars

AND THEY REALLY ARE. First comes a dense chocolate brownie-like base, then a stick-to-your-teeth caramel layer and finally a layer of chopped pecans covered with a drizzle of melted chocolate.

Brownie Layer

3 1-ounce squares semisweet chocolate
3 1-ounce squares unsweetened chocolate
1 cup (2 sticks) unsalted butter, cut into small pieces
¾ cup packed light brown sugar
¾ cup sugar
4 large eggs
1 teaspoon vanilla extract
¾ cup unbleached all-purpose flour
¼ teaspoon salt

Caramel Layer

½ cup (1 stick) unsalted butter
1½ cups packed light brown sugar
½ cup light corn syrup
1 cup heavy cream
1 teaspoon vanilla extract
1½ cups coarsely chopped pecans

Chocolate Drizzles

½ cup semisweet chocolate chips
2 tablespoons unsalted butter
1 tablespoon light corn syrup

1. Preheat the oven to 350 degrees F. Lightly butter and flour a 13-x-9-inch baking pan.

2. **To make the Brownie Layer:** Combine the semisweet and unsweetened chocolates and the butter in a saucepan. Heat over low heat, stirring occasionally, until melted, about 5 minutes. Let stand until cooled.

3. Meanwhile, in a large bowl, beat together the sugars, eggs and vanilla with an electric mixer. Beat on high speed until the mixture is light and foamy, about 10 minutes.

4. Sift together the flour and salt. Fold the chocolate mixture into the egg mixture until blended. Add the flour mixture and stir just to blend.

5. Spread the batter in the prepared pan. Bake for 25 minutes, or until the edges begin to pull away from the sides of the pan. Cool on a wire rack.

6. **To make the Caramel Layer:** Melt the butter in a small, heavy saucepan. Add the brown sugar and corn syrup; heat to boiling. Cook the sugar and corn syrup over medium heat until a candy thermometer registers 240 degrees, or soft-ball stage, about 10 minutes. (If you do not have a candy thermometer, test by dropping a spoonful of the caramel into a cup of cold water; the caramel should form a soft, pliable ball that you can hold between your fingers.) Add the heavy cream all at once. (It will spatter a little.) Continue cooking over medium heat until the thermometer registers 248 degrees, or firm-ball stage, about 25 min-

utes. (If you do not have a candy thermometer, test by dropping a spoonful of water into a cup of cold water; the caramel should form a soft, pliable ball.) Remove from the heat. Add the vanilla and stir to blend. Set the caramel aside to cool to lukewarm, about 30 minutes.

7. Pour the caramel evenly over the cooled brownies, spreading it with a wide spatula. Immediately sprinkle the chopped pecans over the top; press down slightly. Cool thoroughly. (The pan can be refrigerated to keep the caramel firm, if desired.)

8. **To make the Chocolate Drizzles:** When the caramel is cool, heat the chocolate chips, butter and corn syrup over low heat, stirring, until melted. Cool to room temperature. Drizzle the chocolate mixture from the tip of a teaspoon in a random pattern over the top of the caramel-and-pecan layer. Let stand until set. Using a thin sharp knife, cut into bars.

MAKES 24 BARS

Vanilla Shortbread Bars

BUTTERY, DELICATE AND SWEET with vanilla, these bars are a cross between a cookie and shortbread. For an extra-special touch, sprinkle vanilla sugar on top of the baked bars. Having it on hand takes a little planning, but it is worth the effort.

To make Vanilla Sugar:
Tuck a whole vanilla bean in a box or jar of confectioners' or fine granulated sugar and leave it, undisturbed, for at least 2 weeks or longer. The vanilla will gently perfume the sugar. Use vanilla sugar whenever a recipe calls for a dusting of sugar.

1 cup (2 sticks) unsalted butter, softened but not runny
½ cup sifted confectioners' sugar
2 teaspoons vanilla extract

2 cups unbleached all-purpose flour
¼ teaspoon baking powder
¼ teaspoon salt

Vanilla sugar (see previous page)

1. Preheat the oven to 350 degrees F. Lightly butter and flour a 9-inch square pan.

2. Beat the butter and confectioners' sugar until light and creamy, scraping the sides and bottom of the bowl as needed. Blend in the vanilla extract.

3. Sift together the flour, baking powder and salt. Gradually add the flour mixture to the creamed mixture, using a rubber spatula to stir gently and blend until a soft dough forms. Do not overmix.

4. Place the dough between 2 sheets of wax paper. Using a rolling pin, roll out into a thick 9-x-9-inch square, no larger. Remove the top sheet of wax paper and invert the dough into the prepared pan. With floured fingertips, lightly press the dough into the corners of the pan and trim any excess. Peel off and discard the top piece of wax paper.

5. Bake for 5 minutes. Reduce the oven temperature to 300 degrees and bake for 20 to 25 minutes more, or until the edges and top of the shortbread are lightly golden. Cool on a wire rack. Place the vanilla sugar in a small strainer and sprinkle it evenly over the surface before cutting into bars.

MAKES 16 BARS

White & Bittersweet Chocolate Chunk Bars

THESE ARE RICH, moist and scrumptious. White chocolate, which is almost all cocoa butter, provides just the right background for the contrast of the bitter chocolate. The raisins add texture and a fruity flavor. If possible, use a good-quality brand of chocolate, such as Ghirardelli, Lindt or Calle- baut. If those are unavail- able, substitute semisweet chocolate squares.

½ cup (1 stick) unsalted butter

6 ounces white chocolate, chopped into small pieces

3 large eggs

⅔ cup sugar

2 teaspoons vanilla extract

1¼ cups unbleached all-purpose flour

½ cup chopped walnuts

⅓ cup golden raisins

4 ounces bittersweet chocolate, cut into chunks

1. Preheat the oven to 350 degrees F. Lightly butter a 9-inch square pan.

2. Heat the butter in a small, heavy saucepan over low heat until melted. Remove from the heat and add half of the white chocolate; do not stir. Set aside until the white chocolate melts.

3. Meanwhile, in a large bowl, beat the eggs with an electric mixer until frothy. Gradually add the sugar and beat until the mixture is light, about 3 minutes.
Beat in the vanilla.

4. In a separate bowl, combine 2 tablespoons of the flour with the walnuts and raisins; set aside.

5. Add the melted butter and white chocolate and the remaining 1 cup plus 2 tablespoons flour to the beaten eggs; stir to blend. Add the raisin-and-walnut mixture, the remaining chopped white chocolate and the bittersweet chocolate. Stir just until blended.

6. Spread the batter into the prepared pan. Bake for about 30 minutes, or until the edges begin to pull away from the sides of the pan. Cool on a wire rack for at least 3 hours before cutting into bars.

MAKES 18 BARS

Walnut Bars with Chocolate

S O ELEGANT AND BUTTERY, no one will believe how truly quick and easy these are to make. Eat them plain, drizzle them with a little melted chocolate, or coat the surface of each bar entirely with chocolate, as in this recipe. These are even better the second day, so don't hesitate to make them up ahead to have on hand.

Batter

1¼ cups walnut pieces
1¼ cups unbleached all-purpose flour
½ cup packed light brown sugar
½ teaspoon baking powder
 Pinch of salt
½ cup (1 stick) unsalted butter, melted

Chocolate

3 1-ounce squares semisweet chocolate, chopped
2 tablespoons unsalted butter, cut into pieces

1. Preheat the oven to 350 degrees F. Lightly butter a 9-inch square pan.

2. **To make the Batter:** Combine the walnuts, flour, brown sugar, baking powder and salt in the bowl of a food processor. Process until the nuts are finely ground. Add the melted butter through the feed tube; process until the mixture is finely crumbled.

3. Spread the dough evenly into the prepared pan, pressing down with your fingertips. Cut the dough into bars with a table knife. Bake on the center rack for 20 to 25 minutes, or until golden. While the bars are still warm, re-cut them. Cool on a wire rack. Carefully remove from the pan.

4. **To make the Chocolate:** Melt the chocolate and butter in a saucepan over very low heat, without stirring. (Or place in a heatproof bowl and microwave on high, stirring every 30 seconds, until melted, about 2 minutes.) Remove from the heat; stir gently just until blended. Cool slightly. With your fingers, dip the tops of each bar into the chocolate to coat. Return to the wire rack and let stand until the chocolate sets.

MAKES 16 BARS

XOXOs
(Hugs & Kisses)

THESE CHOCOLATE SHORTBREAD BARS are dedicated to a colleague, Lori Longbotham. Whenever I receive any correspondence from Lori, whether it is a letter or a scribbled post-it note, she always pens XOXO and then signs her name. Lori's "hugs and kisses" now grace these squares of dark cocoa shortbread.

Shortbread

1   cup (2 sticks) unsalted butter, softened
1½ cups unbleached all-purpose flour
1   cup sifted confectioners' sugar
1   cup unsweetened cocoa powder, prefer-
    ably imported or European-style
2   teaspoons vanilla extract

Icing

2½ tablespoons unsalted butter, softened
½   cup sifted confectioners' sugar
    About 2 teaspoons milk
⅛   teaspoon almond extract

1. Line a 9-inch square pan with foil. Lightly butter and flour the foil.

2. **To make the Shortbread:** Combine all of the ingredients in a large bowl. Beat with an electric mixer on low speed, scraping the sides and the bottom of the bowl. The mixture will go from dry and crumbly to a dark, moist dough after about 5 minutes of beating.

3. Form the dough into a disc; place the disc between 2 sheets of wax paper. Roll out into a 9-inch square. Lift off the top piece of the wax paper and invert the square into the prepared pan. Peel off and discard the second piece of paper. Press the dough evenly into the corners of the pan and trim any excess from the edges. Cut the dough evenly into bars, 4 across and 4 down. Cover and refrigerate for 1 hour.

4. Preheat the oven to 350 degrees F.

5. Bake the shortbread for 5 minutes. Reduce the heat to 300 degrees. Bake for 25 to 30 minutes more, or until the shortbread begins to pull away from the sides of the pan. Cool on a wire rack for 15 minutes. Re-cut the bars with the tip of a paring knife. Let stand until thoroughly cooled.

6. **To make the Icing:** In a small bowl, beat together the butter and confectioners' sugar with a wooden spoon. Add the milk as needed to form a stiff but smooth icing. Stir in the almond extract.

7. To decorate the shortbread, transfer the icing to a heavy-duty sandwich bag and squeeze it into one corner of the bag. Using scissors, cut a tiny nip from the corner of the bag. Squeeze out a little of the icing to judge the width. You want the icing to make letters that are at least ¼ inch wide. Cut away more if necessary. If the nip in the bag is too large, push the icing over to the other corner of the bag and try again.

8. Using the foil, lift the shortbread out of the pan. Separate into bars and decorate each serving with a large X or a large O.

MAKES 16 BARS

Yogi Bars

I LOVE THE TEXTURE of these bars, very light and just a little chewy, and their rich honey flavor. Try using different types of honey. (My favorites are chestnut and macadamia blossom — not typical, but very, very good.)

½ cup (1 stick) unsalted butter, softened

¼ cup sugar

½ cup honey, plus ¼ cup for the glaze

1 large egg, beaten

1 cup unbleached all-purpose flour

½ teaspoon baking powder

¼ teaspoon baking soda

2 teaspoons grated orange zest

1. Preheat the oven to 350 degrees F. Lightly butter a 9-inch square pan.

2. In a large bowl, beat the butter and sugar with an electric mixer until light. Gradually beat in the ½ cup of honey in a thin, steady stream. Gradually add the egg.

3. Sift together the flour, baking powder and baking soda. Gradually add the dry ingredients to the creamed mixture. Stir in the orange zest.

4. Spread the batter in the prepared pan. Bake for 20 to 25 minutes, or until the edges begin to pull away from the sides of the pan. Cool on a wire rack for 15 minutes.

5. Meanwhile, in a small saucepan over low heat, heat the remaining ¼ cup honey until very runny. Lightly brush it over the top of the bars. Cool thoroughly before cutting into bars.

MAKES 16 BARS

Zebra Bars

INVARIABLY, when I mentioned to friends that I was busy organizing my bar cookie ideas alphabetically, someone would ask about the letter Z. The truth is, I have known about chocolate-and-white-striped Zebra Bars as long as I have known about bars made with applesauce, almonds or apricots. Z was as easy as A. And as scrumptious.

1½ **cups semisweet chocolate chips**	1 **cup packed light brown sugar**
2 **cups unbleached all-purpose flour**	2 **large eggs**
1 **teaspoon baking powder**	1 **teaspoon vanilla extract**
1 **cup (2 sticks) unsalted butter, softened**	¾ **cup chopped walnuts**

1. Preheat the oven to 350 degrees F. Lightly butter a 13-x-9-inch baking pan.

2. Melt 1 cup of the chocolate chips in a small saucepan over low heat; cool slightly. (Or place the chocolate in a heatproof bowl and microwave on high, stirring every 30 seconds, until melted, about 2 minutes.) Set aside.

3. Sift together the flour and baking powder; set aside. In a large bowl, beat the butter and the brown sugar with an electric mixer until light and fluffy. Beat in the eggs, one at a time,

beating thoroughly after each addition; beat in the vanilla. Stir in the sifted ingredients until blended.

4. Transfer half of the batter to a second bowl. Stir the melted chocolate into one portion until blended. Spread the chocolate batter in the prepared pan. Drop the remaining batter by tablespoonfuls onto the chocolate batter. Spread carefully into an even layer. Sprinkle with the remain-

ing ½ cup chocolate chips and the walnuts.

5. Bake on the center rack for 30 minutes, or until the edges begin to pull away from the sides of the pan. Cool in the pan on a wire rack before cutting into bars.

MAKES 24 BARS

Index